in

# Ohio's Western Reserve

## Discovering nature and history in the northeastern corner

## JAY ABERCROMBIE

Backcountry Publications
Woodstock · Vermont

**An invitation to the reader**

If you find that conditions have changed along these walks, please let the author and publisher know so that corrections may be made in future printings. Address all correspondence to:

Editor, Walks and Rambles™ Series
Backcountry Publications
PO Box 748
Woodstock, Vermont 05091

**Library of Congress Cataloging-in-Publication Data**
Abercrombie, Jay
    Walks and rambles in Ohio's Western Reserve : discovering nature and history in the northeastern corner / Jay Abercrombie.
      p.  cm.
    ISBN 0-88150-285-5 (alk. paper)
    1. Walking—Ohio—Western Reserve—Guidebooks. 2. Western Reserve (Ohio)—Guidebooks.
    I. Title.
GV199.42.O32W473     1996
917.71'3—dc20                       95-43394
                                        CIP

Published by Backcountry Publications
A division of The Countryman Press
PO Box 748
Woodstock, VT 05091

Distributed by W.W. Norton & Company, Inc.
500 Fifth Avenue
New York, NY 10110

Printed in Canada

Cover and text design by Sally Sherman
Maps by Alex Wallach, © 1996 The Countryman Press
Cover photo by the Ohio Department of Natural Resources
All photographs by the author, unless otherwise credited

*For my mother*

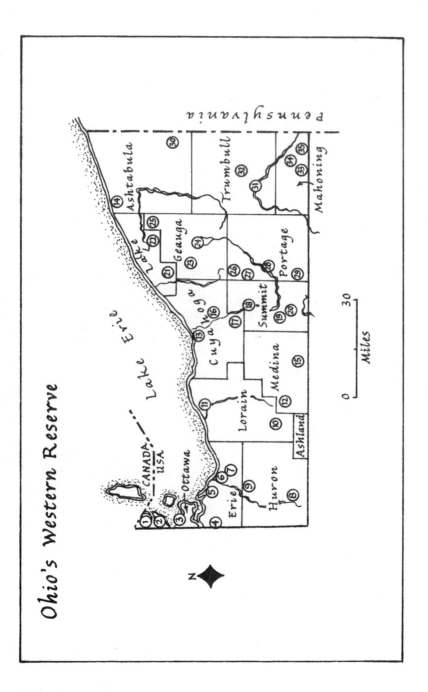

*Ohio's Western Reserve*

# Contents

# Acknowledgments

For their assistance in providing information and advice, I am especially grateful to Christine Ashby, Judy Barnhart, Jim Bauder, Sharon Bezoski, Tom Bresko, Beth Buchanan, Anne Bugeda, Doug Burgett, Carl Cassevecha, Jane Christyson, Steve Coles, Kim Coy, Todd Crandall, Nancy Fulton, Jonathan Granville, Ed Isaly, Paul Kammermeier, Jeff Kest, Paul Labovitz, Wendell Lauth, Linda Lewis, Lachlan Mackay, Laura Mataraza, Dan Melcher, Carol Poh Miller, John Olive, Ralph Ramey, Paul Saldutte, Virginia Shaw, Tom Stanley, Walter Starcher, Patty Stevens, Mike Whitham, and Gene Wright.

Special thanks must go to those who contributed most to the book's completion: the photographer, Beverly J. Brown; the people of Backcountry Publications (particularly Robin Dutcher-Bayer, Margaret Hanshaw, Laura Jorstad, Carl Taylor, Doris Troy, Betsy Walker, and Helen Whybrow); and my daughters Co and Chau. Without them, this guide would not have been possible.

# Introduction

**O**hio's Western Reserve is a historically distinctive region in the northeastern corner of the Buckeye State. The Reserve, an endearing region of fertile plains and rolling hills, lies along Lake Erie in the very heart of North America where the cultures of the Midwest and the East Coast, the North and the South, meet. The Western Reserve also is located in an ecological transition zone, and the area's wild places abound with a rich and varied flora and fauna. The natural attractions combine with cultural and historic sites, making for delightful and memorable journeys to explore human and natural history.

Novelist Louis Bromfield said, "Ohio is the farthest west of the east and the farthest north of the south." He was speaking in a cultural sense, but his observation is true biologically as well, about both the state and the Western Reserve. The Reserve is the northernmost land in Ohio and stretches along the southern shore of the southernmost Great Lake. It lies at the western edge of the mountains and the eastern fringe of the plains. Its location makes it home to western as well as eastern species, northern as well as southern members of the biota.

Measured in size, the Western Reserve covers only a small part of the state and the nation, but it encompasses an astonishing variety of geography and beautiful scenery—from serene to breathtaking. It extends west from Pennsylvania for 120 miles, varying in width from 25 to 67 miles. The Reserve consists of nine counties—Ashtabula, Cuyahoga, Geauga, Huron, Lake, Lorain, Medina, Portage, and Trumbull—and parts of five additional counties—Ashland, Erie, Mahoning, Ottawa, and Summit.

What eventually became known as the Western Reserve had its origins in England in 1662, before any Englishman had ever set foot on the land. In that year, King Charles II granted a royal charter to the colony of Connecticut. The description of Connecticut's New World holdings was vague and conflicted with other land grants already established, not to mention the French claims and Native rights to the land, but the colony seemed to extend westward from near Narragansett Bay to "the South Sea" (the Pacific Ocean).

After the American Revolution, England ceded the land north of the Ohio River and west of the Appalachian Mountains—the Northwest Territory—to the United States. The new Congress persuaded the individual states to surrender their old claims to the western lands. All agreed, except Connecticut. In 1786, Connecticut finally gave up her land from Lake Erie to the Pacific, but she reserved a swath in the Ohio country that extended west from Pennsylvania for 120 miles between 41 degrees and 42 degrees, 2 minutes north latitude (Connecticut's south and north boundaries). With almost 4700 square miles, the reserve was nearly as large as the mother state. The territory was called New Connecticut, but became known as The Connecticut Reserve or The Connecticut Western Reserve. In legal and historical documents it is The Western Reserve of Connecticut, but in Ohio it is simply called the Western Reserve.

The Connecticut General Assembly in 1795 formed a committee to sell the state's western holdings. The proceeds of the sale were to be placed in a special perpetual fund, the interest from which was to be used for the support of the Connecticut schools. The fund is still in effect. The committee sold the entire Western Reserve to a kind of syndicate by the name of the Connecticut Land Company for $1.2 million—about 48 cents an acre. Before turning over the land to the speculators, the General Assembly formed a separate reserve within the Western Reserve by setting aside almost 800 square miles in its westernmost part for those Connecticut citizens whose homes and properties were burned by the British during the Revolution. This region was known in Connecticut as the Sufferers' Lands and in Ohio as the Firelands.

The Connecticut Land Company sent a surveying party to the Western Reserve in 1796 to measure off 5-square-mile townships and further subdivide the land into ranges and sections. The land grid is still in place, giving the Western Reserve a different political geography map from the rest of Ohio.

The Connecticut settlers brought not only their system of land planning, but their New England architecture, Yankee viewpoints, and

*Trillium blossoms brighten the woodlands of the Western Reserve each spring.*

Puritan values as well. James A. Garfield, a Western Reserve native who was a scholar and educator before he entered politics, noted in an address before the Geauga County Historical Society in 1873 that the pioneers "planted the institutions and opinions of old Connecticut in their wilderness homes [and] nourished them with an energy and devotion scarcely equalled in any other quarter of the world."

Alfred Mathews wrote one of the first histories of the Western Reserve in 1902 and observed "the fact that the pioneers . . . planted in the New Connecticut of the Western Reserve . . . the last organized and distinct colony of Puritanism." Historian P.P. Cherry wrote in 1920: "The Western Reserve has a character and an individuality of its own that is not found in any other section of our country. It is really a state within a state."

Tremendous changes swept over the Western Reserve in the decades following Cherry's book. Great new manufacturing complexes in the automotive, rubber, and steel industries attracted workers from overseas and from the American South. Strong in community spirit and tolerant of others' viewpoints, the newcomers changed the ethnic fiber of the Reserve while adding a new dimension to self-reliance, the hallmark Yankee trait. The Western Reserve absorbed the new arrivals and retained its Yankee quality to a substantial degree. Ohio scholar and historian Harlan Hatcher, writing in the middle of the 20th century, concluded: "In spite of all that has happened . . . the Reserve is still different from the rest of Ohio."

Today, at the end of the 20th century, 200 years after the first white settlements, the old character of the Western Reserve is increasingly difficult to find. The unique cultural features of the Western Reserve—the architecture, the landmarks, the New England lifestyle— have largely succumbed to expanding industrialism and changing customs. Sprawling urbanism threatens what little is left, with garden apartments and shopping malls rising up in every meadow and corn- field. Yet the old ways linger if you look carefully. Historian Eric J. Cardinal maintained in 1988: "No one would argue that the Western Reserve remains a bastion of Yankee Puritanism in the last quarter of the twentieth century." Roger J. Kennedy, director of the National Museum of American History of the Smithsonian Institution, wrote in 1989 of the remarkable concentration of Greek Revival architec- ture—evidence of New England influence—in the Western Reserve, and even noted a distinctive glottal speech pattern typical of Yankees that persists in the region.

In the Western Reserve natural history and human history are intertwined—as they always have been in the unfolding story of the world and its people striving to find harmony with their surround- ings. The Reserve is a great meeting place for several distinct physi- ographic, climatic, vegetational, and faunal elements. The result is a remarkably rich diversity of plants and animals. Over 2000 species of plants are found in the Western Reserve. With this rich plant life comes an equally varied fauna. The migrant bird life is especially impressive, with wood warblers and other songbirds in the forests and thickets, and ducks, geese, grebes, and shorebirds in the marshes and along Lake Erie.

· An obvious natural division of the Western Reserve is into watersheds. The Reserve straddles the Continental Divide, with some rivers flowing north to Lake Erie and eventually emptying into the North Atlantic Ocean via the St. Lawrence River. Other waterways flow south toward the Ohio River, reaching the Gulf of Mexico by way of the Mississippi River.

The Western Reserve is also divided naturally into three physiographic provinces: the Lake Plains, the Till Plains, and the Allegheny Plateau.

Lying along Lake Erie at the northern edge of the Western Reserve are the Lake Plains, noteworthy for their flatness. Narrow in the east, the Lake Plains broaden to extend more than 16 miles inland from the lake near Sandusky Bay in the west. Forests on the plains are good places to find hackberry, a warty-barked tree in the elm family that has a rather wide geographic range but flourishes in the midlands. Marshes along the lake harbor a wide assortment of waterfowl and wading birds. In the west, isolated prairies are interspersed among the forests. A few prairie plants and insects reach their easternmost localities in the Western Reserve. On the sandy dunes near the lake are found some grasses that grow elsewhere only on the beaches of the Atlantic Ocean or the Gulf of Mexico. The Lake Plains received the region's first white explorers and settlers. Early towns sprang up along the shore and today they rank among the state's leading cities. In among the marshes, prairies, and cities are vineyards, orchards, and nursery farms.

An arrowlike wedge of the Till Plains enters the Western Reserve from the southwest and reaches eastward to beyond the Rocky River. The Till Plains are more undulating and gently sloping than the Lake Plains, although the boundary between the two regions is sometimes indistinct. The Till Plains harbor unusual southern relic species such as some rare butterflies and tall pawpaw, the only North American member of the tropical custard-apple family. The Till Plains are dotted with prosperous farms and small, agrarian communities. The fertile agricultural land is interspersed with isolated wild areas preserved along creeks and rivers or set aside as state parks and wildlife areas.

In the eastern part of the Western Reserve, the landscape changes dramatically. Here is a region of rounded, rolling hills and deep valleys—the Appalachian Plateau, called the Allegheny Plateau in Ohio. The Reserve's highest elevations (more than 1300 feet) occur here. In places, outcrops of sandstone rise in spectacular cliffs called ledges. Northern bogs on the plateau have American larch, leather-leaf, and a host of other specialized plants. The forests of the hill country house such northern trees as eastern hemlock, yellow birch, and white pine, as well as such southern species as tulip tree and black gum. Large urban centers, green-pastured dairy farms, and parcels of dense beech and maple woods are found on the rolling plateau, along with open meadows and old fields.

The joining of two major watersheds and three vast physiographic provinces in the Western Reserve makes for the diversity of plants and animals that ecologists would expect to find. But the richness is increased even more by other land forms that brush close to the Reserve, or are near enough so that there are no significant migratory barriers to the dispersal of species. To the east and southeast, the lumpish Allegheny Plateau rises to the Appalachian Mountains; to the west stretch the central plains of the interior. Not far north is the boreal forest of the Canadian Shield, and to the northeast, via Lake Ontario and the St. Lawrence River, is the Atlantic Coast. Each of these places has its own unique plants and animals, and here the edges of the ranges of these species come together to form varied communities.

The hikes in this book reach into virtually every available habitat in the Western Reserve: upland forests of American beech, sugar maple, red oak, white oak, shagbark hickory, and basswood; lowland forests of American elm, red maple, pin oak, swamp white oak, and green ash; floodplain forests of American sycamore, silver maple, cottonwood, and box-elder; prairies of big bluestem, little bluestem, Indian grass, and prairie-dock; brushland; meadows; marshes; swamps; old fields; islands in Lake Erie; sandy and cobbly beaches; sand dunes; rocky cliffs; and human-made environments such as ponds, reservoirs, a canal, former railroads, old carriageways, agricultural lands, and urban historic districts.

The pathways follow threads of history running back from the present to before written narratives began: memories of the Hopewell; bloody-handed French fur traders; gentle yet tough Moravian missionaries; Connecticut Yankees; brave seamen; boisterous "canawlers";

refuge-seeking Mormons; powerful industrialists; impassioned social reformers; steel workers from Europe; and rubber workers from the South.

## How To Use This Book

This trail guide is divided into two geographical areas: The Plains (including both the Lake Plains and the Till Plains) and The Plateau. Both regions offer a wide variety of scenery and unique characteristics, an unexpected surprise for such a relatively small area.

Each chapter provides a complete description of a hike, detailed instructions on how to reach the trailhead from a nearby town, and a commentary on the area's natural or human history. A capsule highlight of what can be seen is provided at the beginning of each hike's description, along with the distance and an estimated hiking time. The latter figure is an average that tries to allow for personal preferences.

Also listed at the outset you will find the United States Geological Survey (USGS) 7.5-minute quadrangle map or maps showing the area of the hike. When available, other maps (such as those published by state parks) that show the area or the trails are also listed. All these maps are mentioned only to provide the hiker with more detailed information if desired. They are not specifically needed to follow the trails, since sketch maps of each hike are pictured in the book. On these latter maps, the following standard map symbols are used:

parking Ⓟ
main trail ● ● ● ●
side trail • • •
viewpoint

Hiking in the Western Reserve is possible during all four seasons. Some of the trails in this book also can be skied or snowshoed in winter. If walking or snowshoeing on a ski trail, stay to either side so that you do not disturb the ski tracks in the snow. Many people find winter the ideal season to be on the trail because they avoid the crowds and biting insects of summer. Warm-weather walks, on the other hand, can be especially scenic and pleasant. Summer is rich with color and activity in nature, while spring and autumn offer the vibrant changes in which all living things become immersed.

## The Trails

Most of the hikes in this book are along marked and maintained trails. The majority of the trails are easy and safe, but some of the pathways are covered with water in the spring and after heavy rains. Wear footgear you do not mind getting wet or muddy. Carry insect repellent in your pack in case mosquitoes, deerflies, or blackflies become bothersome. Poison ivy is common; ticks are rare. The only poisonous snake remaining in the Western Reserve is the eastern massasauga. This rattlesnake is an endangered species in Ohio; your chances of encountering one are close to zero. Disjunct populations of timber rattlesnakes formerly occurred on some of the Erie Islands and the Catawba Island and Marblehead Peninsulas, but the species was eradicated and no sightings have occurred in the Reserve since the 1950s.

Running across the Western Reserve and featured as part of several hikes is the Buckeye Trail, a 1200-mile circuit that loops around Ohio. Northeast Ohio is a good region to walk this trail, since there is an inner loop that passes through many of the Western Reserve's natural areas. For more information, contact the Buckeye Trail Association, PO Box 254, Worthington, OH 43085.

The Western Reserve is a wonderful place to explore on foot. Walking is one of the favorite pastimes of Reserve residents. Hiking events held by the Lorain County Metropolitan Park District and Metro Parks, Serving Summit County have thousands of participants each year. A 1992 survey by Lake Metroparks found that walking was "the most commonly desired activity that park users expect to enjoy." David B. Cooper, editor of the *Akron Beacon Journal,* wrote in 1993: "Such amenities as . . . hiking trails . . . add greatly to everyone's quality of life." The lure of walking through woods, by streams, and along city and village paths remains and is being discovered by more enthusiasts every year. As a result, new trails are being developed and old trails are being improved to provide more and better recreational opportunities. The story of the Western Reserve, its people, and its trails is an unfinished book.

On a few of the walks and rambles, you will come across small, pearly white, quartz pebbles—"lucky stones," we call them in the Western Reserve. They have eroded out of the 300-million-year-old sandstone bedrock that underlies much of the Reserve. Look for them, tread respectfully here and elsewhere, and take time to pick up one or two to add to your pack or pocket. They fetch good medicine, safe travel, long memory.

# The Plains

*Old Woman Creek (Beverly J. Brown)*

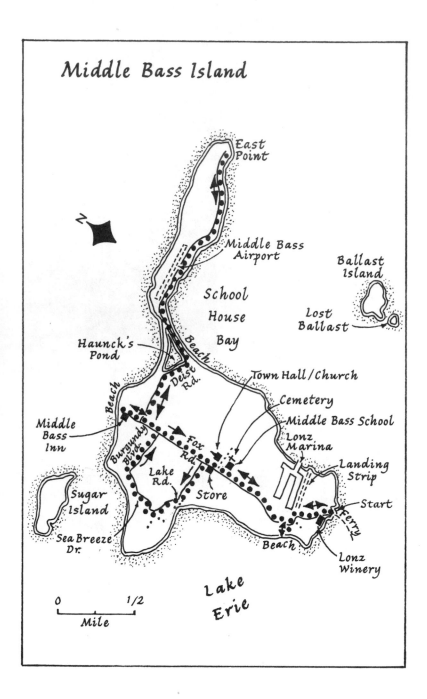

# Middle Bass Island

East Point

Middle Bass Airport

School House Bay

Ballast Island

Lost Ballast

Haunck's Pond

Beach

Deisy Rd.

Town Hall / Church

Cemetery

Middle Bass School

Lonz Marina

Middle Bass Inn

Beach

Burgundy Blvd.

Fox Rd.

Landing Strip

Lake Rd.

Store

Start

Sugar Island

Sea Breeze Dr.

Beach

Ferry

Lonz Winery

0      1/2

Mile

Lake Erie

# Middle Bass Island

### Boat excursion and walking on one of Lake Erie's Bass Islands

*Hiking distance: 8¼ miles*
*Hiking time: 4 hours*
*Map: USGS Put-in-Bay*

In western Lake Erie lies an archipelago of low, limestone islands. Like giant stepping stones between Ohio and Ontario, the main islands hopscotch across the lake from the Catawba Island and Marblehead Peninsulas on the south shore to Point Pelee in Canada. Twenty-one of the islands are large enough to have names, but a number of islets and rocky reefs are nameless.

The Lake Erie islands are formed of solid limestone rock. The western basin of the lake is more shallow than the eastern end because the Pleistocene glacier encountered a more formidable barrier in the stratum of limestone in the west compared to the easily eroded Devonian sandstone in the east. Hence, this portion of the lake was less deeply excavated by the ice. The more prominent or most resistant masses of limestone were left and now project as islands above the water. The channels separating the islands are only between about 22 and 30 feet deep.

Prominent among the islands on the American side are the three Bass Islands, referring, of course, to the great numbers of fish of that name always found in the surrounding water. The central island, Middle Bass Island, lies about 6 miles from the Catawba Island Peninsula, the nearest point on the mainland. It is about ½ mile from South Bass and about 1 mile from North Bass. It is not only middle in location, but also middle in size, with a total area of 1.2 square miles. The low-slung island is nearly flat, rising less than 25 feet above lake level.

*The small and graceful Bonaparte's gull (Beverly J. Brown)*

Middle Bass was apparently the first of the Erie islands to be visited by white men. In 1679 the French vessel *Griffin*, captained by explorer René Robert Cavelier, Sieur de la Salle, with missionary Father Louis Hennepin on board, sailed west across Lake Erie. They reached the archipelago and came ashore on Middle Bass, where Hennepin conducted a Mass and La Salle took possession in the name of His Most Christian Majesty, King Louis XIV. The French were "enchanted by the floral beauty" and named it Île des Fleurs.

The British ultimately gained control of Lake Erie, but they relinquished the Bass Islands after the American Revolution. In 1807, Alfred Pierpont Edwards purchased Middle Bass and other islands from the Connecticut Land Company and began to evict the French-Canadians, whom he considered as squatters. The British returned to Lake Erie at the onset of the War of 1812 and renewed their claims to all the islands. At the end of the war, as a result of the Treaty of Ghent, the British permanently gave up all claims to the Bass Islands.

There are no parks or other public lands on Middle Bass Island. This hike explores the island by following county and township roads and occasionally reaches Lake Erie on small, secluded beaches.

## Access

Public transportation directly from the mainland to Middle Bass Island is provided daily in season by Miller Boat Line from the Catawba Island Peninsula (419-285-2421). Sonny S Water Taxi offers daily direct service from Put-in-Bay on South Bass Island (419-285-8774 or 419-285-4631). Our walk starts at the ferry dock on the south side of the island. Ferry access to Middle Bass on weekdays before Memorial Day and after Labor Day is limited. Plan your trip by calling any of the numbers above.

Griffing Island Airlines flies to Middle Bass Airport on East Point from the Marblehead Peninsula and from Sandusky. Call 419-734-3149 for flight information. Private boats can dock at Lonz Marina on the east shore of Middle Bass.

## Trail

From the ferry dock, take the flagstone path through stone columns opposite the ticket office and enter the grounds of Lonz Winery, punctuated with red cedars and large hackberry trees. Leave the path and walk diagonally left across the grass toward picnic tables and volleyball courts. The open slope provides ideal foraging areas for chimney swifts, swallows, and purple martins. The winery is on your left. Beneath the fanciful Gothic building are hand-hewn limestone wine cellars, dug out about 1865 by the Golden Eagle Winery and today on the National Register of Historic Places. Peter Lonz took over the operation in 1884. Tours of the building and cellars are offered daily in the afternoons between May 15 and September 26; additional evening tours are conducted on Friday and Saturday between Memorial Day and Labor Day.

Reach the volleyball courts at the top of the slope and continue straight on a gravel lane with a small vineyard on the left and a house on the right. Cross a gravel lane and leave the winery property.

Approach the Lonz Marina, which offers dockage for private boats. The docks and pilings around the marina are favored places to find Bonaparte's gulls. Just before you reach the marina, turn left on a gravel lane that doubles as a landing strip. Cross paved Fox Road and continue straight on a track to reach a little beach of wave-worn cobbles and polished driftwood. The vantage point provides out-standing views to the west of Lake Erie. Islands visible are (from left to right) South Bass and Gibraltar, Green, and Rattlesnake. On clear days you can see the low mainland resting on the far horizon.

Walk back to Fox Road and turn left. Pass on your right the white frame Middle Bass School, a one-room structure built in the late 1860s. The last classes were held in the building in 1982. The island's four school-age children now go by boat taxi or airplane to Put-in-Bay schools on South Bass. The island cemetery is behind the school-house.

The next building on the right as you walk along Fox Road is the 1877 town hall, used by the Church of Middle Bass on Sunday. The general store is on your left. Turn left past the store onto a paved side street. The road leads through a forest of hackberry, mulberry, cottonwood, and silver maple before reaching old fields and then a residential area. Fork right on paved Lake Road.

Turn right at the next crossroad (Sea Breeze Drive), a narrow, paved lane. The way curves right, then left as it passes through a development of summer homes and cottages. Near the lake, pass the Burgundy Bay Club as the drive curves right and becomes Burgundy Boulevard. Come out onto Fox Road again and turn left.

Deist Road soon goes to the right, but continue straight to the end of Fox Road to visit another small beach on the north shore of the island. The Middle Bass Inn sits on a picturesque cobble shore, with good views of the lake and green-mantled islands. Rattlesnake Island, with its two rocky islets, The Rattles, trailing behind, can be seen just off the point to your left. (An interesting bit of Western Reserve trivia is that Rattlesnake is in the Reserve, but The Rattles are not; the Reserve's western boundary passes just west of the "tail" of Rattlesnake and cuts off The Rattles). Sugar Island is close by at about 10 o'clock and North Bass is the big island to the north.

Turn around and walk south on Fox Road. To explore the east side of Middle Bass, turn left on Deist Road. You reach a narrow neck connecting the main bulk of the island with East Point. On the left is Haunck's Pond, a rich wetland filled with bulrush, cattails, arrow-heads, sedges, water-lilies, American lotus, spatterdock, vervain, buttonbush, cottonwood, and willows. Insect hunters—dragonflies and swallows—are common here. The pond represents the juncture of what were formerly two islands (the main island behind you and the East Point area ahead). Gravel bars formed between the two islands and eventually joined them.

Where the way curves sharply left there is a pleasant beach straight ahead on School House Bay, reached by climbing over a wall of riprap. Deist Road goes through a canyon of riprap, with large rocks placed along both sides of the road to keep the two parts of Middle Bass from becoming separated again.

As the road curves right toward East Point, School House Bay, with Ballast Island sitting at its far side, comes into view. You can also see Lost Ballast, a tiny islet that was formerly connected with Ballast but years ago was severed by heavy storms. South Bass can also be seen from here. The Middle Bass Airport is a grass landing strip behind the houses on the left. Reach the end of Deist Road near East Point. The international boundary lies about 2 miles off Middle Bass. Pelee Island, the largest island in the lake, is in Canadian waters to the northeast. Middle Island, a small island lying just 1800 feet north of the border, can be seen to the east. It is the most southerly land in Canada.

Return to Fox Road, turn left, and walk back to the dock near Lonz Winery.

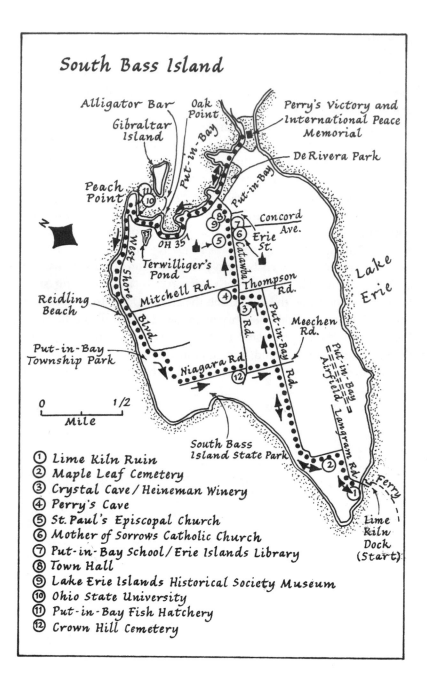

# South Bass Island

Alligator Bar
Oak Point
Gibraltar Island
Peach Point
Put-in-Bay
Perry's Victory and International Peace Memorial
De Rivera Park
Concord Ave.
Erie St.
Put-in-Bay
OH 357
Terwilliger's Pond
Reidling Beach
West Shore Blvd.
Mitchell Rd.
Thompson Rd.
Catawba
Rd.
Put-in-Bay Township Park
Niagara Rd.
Meechen Rd.
Lake Erie
Put-in-Bay = Airfield
Langram Rd.
South Bass Island State Park
Ferry
Lime Kiln Dock (Start)

0        1/2
Mile

① Lime Kiln Ruin
② Maple Leaf Cemetery
③ Crystal Cave / Heineman Winery
④ Perry's Cave
⑤ St. Paul's Episcopal Church
⑥ Mother of Sorrows Catholic Church
⑦ Put-in-Bay School / Erie Islands Library
⑧ Town Hall
⑨ Lake Erie Islands Historical Society Museum
⑩ Ohio State University
⑪ Put-in-Bay Fish Hatchery
⑫ Crown Hill Cemetery

# South Bass Island

## War and peace on Lake Erie

*Hiking distance: 7 miles*
*Hiking time: 3½ hours*
*Map: USGS Put-in-Bay*

The towering memorial on South Bass Island commemorates the naval victory of Master Commandant Oliver Hazard Perry over the British fleet in the Battle of Lake Erie during the War of 1812 and the enduring peace between the United States and Canada that resulted after the conflict.

Perry's victory in 1813 is one of the most significant events in American military history. The War of 1812 was fought on several fronts, and in the Northwest the United States was pressed hard by Great Britain and her Indian allies. The tribes were united under the leadership of the great Shawnee war chief Tecumseh. Detroit had fallen to the British army in 1812. Indians raided the frontier, wiping out the small settlement along Cold Creek near present-day Castalia and massacring the prisoners taken during the Battle of the River Raisin in Michigan. William Henry Harrison, commander of operations in the Northwest, held Fort Meigs (today's Perrysburg) against repeated attacks, but his lines of supply and communication remained tenuous.

The chief reason for the early American failures in the Lake Erie region was America's disregard for British sea power. Britain seized all American ships on the lake and added them to her Lake Erie navy when war broke out. The British armada, commanded by Captain Robert Heriot Barclay, had six vessels with a total armament of 63 guns. To challenge this might, President James Madison decided to increase American naval power on Lake Erie. He commissioned men and money to assemble a fleet of warships that would be able to defeat the British.

Oliver Hazard Perry spent the first months of the war running routine gunboat patrols out of Newport, Rhode Island. Eager for the glory of battle, he readily volunteered to lead the American fleet being built on the lake. Arriving in Erie, Pennsylvania, in March 1813, Perry threw himself into the cause. His primary task became persuading his commanding officer, Commodore Isaac Chauncey, based at Sackett's Harbor, New York, to provide crews for his ships. On July 18, Perry wrote Chauncey: "Give me men, Sir, and I will acquire both for you and myself glory and honor on this lake or perish in the attempt." Chauncey responded by sending a trickle of untrained and sickly men, many of whom had never served aboard a ship. Perry described them as "a motley set."

Despite these and other obstacles, including a blockade by Barclay, Perry managed to get 10 ships with 54 guns under sail in August. The vessels, hastily built of green wood and sailed by a green crew, headed west. The fleet and sailors were assembled with but one aim: to fight a do-or-die battle with the British. Perry trained his men in repetitive drills for the coming engagement. He anchored in Put-in-Bay behind the cover of Gibraltar Island and waited for the British to make the next move. Barclay stuck close to the Canadian shore below the protective guns of Fort Malden at Amherstburg. Perry received his final complement of men when Harrison sent 100 sharpshooters to pick off British officers and crew when the ships should finally close.

Perry named his 20-gun flagship *Lawrence* after his close friend James Lawrence, who had been killed in the Atlantic months before while commanding the frigate *Chesapeake*. Lawrence's dying orders were "Don't give up the ship" and Perry emblazoned these words in muslin letters on a blue background as his battle flag. "When the flag is hoisted to the main royal masthead," Perry instructed his officers, "it shall be your signal for going into action."

As dawn broke on September 10, American lookouts saw British sails approaching from the northwest. Perry weighed anchor and sailed out to meet the oncoming armada.

Perry hoisted his battle flag and the American ships began forming a battle line, with the *Lawrence* in the van. Tension mounted as the ships neared. Seaman David Bunnell of the *Lawrence* recalled:

"My pulse beat quick—all nature seemed wrapped in awful suspense—the dart of death hung as [if] it were trembling by a single hair, and no one knew on whose head it would fall."

Barclay, aboard the 19-gun *Detroit,* began firing his long cannons. The *Lawrence* was the first ship hit. Perry continued to stand down, but his ship and crew endured a murderous fire before the *Lawrence,* with her smaller guns, could come within range of the *Detroit.* The *Lawrence* hung on for two hours despite fierce British broadsides that battered both ship and crew. Perry later wrote, ". . . every gun was rendered useless, and the greater part of her crew killed or wounded." Only 20 out of the *Lawrence's* 103 men were fit for duty.

Perry then made his dramatic dash from the *Lawrence.* Lowering his "Don't Give Up the Ship" flag, and taking the only undamaged rowboat left aboard, he and four sailors rowed through the battle to the *Niagara,* a 20-gun brig that had lagged behind. Hoisting his battle flag to the topmast, Perry pressed the *Niagara* forward to the British line, firing as he came.

The British had also sustained heavy casualties. Barclay, already wounded, was hit again and had to be carried below decks. By the time the *Niagara* had pierced the British battle line the captain and first lieutenant of every British ship was either killed or wounded. Junior officers, attempting to turn the ships to face the onslaught of the *Niagara,* entangled the bow of the 17-gun *Queen Charlotte* with the rigging of the *Detroit.* Perry sailed into the British line and opened up with all his guns from both sides of the *Niagara.* The sharpshooters raked the British decks with rifles and pistols. The British stood this withering fire for 10 minutes, then struck their flags, and all guns ceased firing.

Perry lowered his battle flag and returned to the *Lawrence.* He raised the banner once more and received the formal British surrender on the littered and blood-soaked quarterdeck. Perry scribbled a note to Harrison on the back of an envelope: "We have met the enemy and they are ours. Two ships, two brigs, one schooner and one sloop." It is the only time in history an entire British fleet had been captured.

On the shore, settlers, soldiers, and warriors anxiously awaited the news. No one at any time was unaware of the importance of this battle. The roar of the cannons was heard as far east along the Ohio shore as Madison and as far inland as Ravenna, more than 100 miles away. On the south shore, Harrison waited, knowing full well that the fate of the West hung on the outcome. On the north shore, Major General Henry A. Proctor and Tecumseh waited, perhaps even more concerned. Proctor knew all too well that Harrison would attack Detroit and Fort Malden if Barclay did not destroy the American naval squadron. As the firing ceased and the ships sailed off toward Put-in-Bay instead of returning to Fort Malden, Proctor knew his supply lines were cut and Lake Erie was controlled by the Americans. He hastily abandoned Fort Malden and Detroit and retreated eastward. The enraged Tecumseh, who wanted to stand and fight, called Proctor "a fat animal, that carries its tail upon its back, but when affrighted . . . drops it between his legs and runs off."

The Americans suffered 27 men killed and 96 wounded; the British lost 41 killed and 92 wounded.

The Battle of Lake Erie was one of the few American successes in a war noted for its blunders. The victory helped persuade the British to cease hostilities and enabled the United States to claim the Northwest at the peace talks in Ghent a year later. From the Treaty of Ghent came the Rush-Bagot Agreement signed in 1816. That agreement, which is still in effect, limits the number of warships on Lake Erie to two vessels "not exceeding 100 tons burden, and armed with one 18 lb. cannon."

The Rush-Bagot Agreement was strained during the American Civil War, but it paved the way for the permanent disarmament of the border that now stretches nearly 6000 miles from the Atlantic to the arctic. In the middle is Lake Erie, lying beneath Canada's soft underbelly and arrowing into America's heartland. For almost two centuries, the two nations have shared common beliefs and a continent, separated by little more than a line on a map.

## Access

You can reach South Bass Island by a choice of ferries or airplane. The hike described here starts at Lime Kiln Dock on the south shore of the island where Miller Boat Line arrives daily from the Catawba Island Peninsula (419-285-2421). Put-in-Bay Airfield is on Langram

Road near Lime Kiln Dock. Griffing Island Airlines flies in from the Marblehead Peninsula or Sandusky. Call 419-734-3149 for flight information.

Daily ferry service is provided to downtown Put-in-Bay from Port Clinton (Put-in-Bay Boat Line Company, 800-245-1538) and Middle Bass Island (Sonny S Water Taxi, 419-285-8774 or 419-285-4631). Ferry access to South Bass on weekdays before Memorial Day and after Labor Day is limited. Plan your trip in advance. Private boats can dock at the village wharf in Put-in-Bay or at the state slips at Oak Point Picnic Area.

## Trail

The ruin on the left near the ferry dock is an old lime kiln dating from the 1860s. The island's limestone was burned to produce lime for mortar in local buildings. Walk up from the dock and turn right on Langram Road. Go left at the first opportunity on Put-in-Bay Road and pass Maple Leaf Cemetery on your left. Follow the road as it curves around and then enters a long straightaway. Cross Meechen Road and come to a T-intersection with Thompson Road; turn left.

Go a short distance to the next T-intersection with Catawba Road and turn right. Crystal Cave and Heineman Winery are on your left at this junction. Perry's Cave is across Catawba Road. About 25 small caves are found on South Bass; Crystal and Perry's are the only two open to the public.

Pass Mitchell Road on your left. Enter the village of Put-in-Bay, marked by Saint Paul's Episcopal Church (1865) on the left and Mother of Sorrows Catholic Church (1927), next to a memorial carillon, on the right. The Put-in-Bay School and Erie Islands Library is on the right at the corner of Concord Avenue. The school has grades K through 12 and educates the children from all the Erie Islands in Ottawa County. The graduating class typically has seven students, all of whom usually go on to college. The school also has a program for exchange students from abroad.

Catawba Road curves left where Erie Street goes right. On the left is the town hall (1887) and, behind it, the Lake Erie Islands Historical Society Museum. Those interested in more historic and

*Perry's Victory and International Peace Memorial*

architectural details can purchase a small guidebook, *Put-in-Bay Walking Guide to Historic Buildings,* at the museum.

Pass Delaware Street and DeRivera Park on your right and come to a T-intersection with OH 357 (Bay View Avenue) at the bayfront. Turn right and walk either through the park or along the water. The pyramid of cannonballs in the park marks the grave site of three American and three British officers killed in the Battle of Lake Erie. All of the other fatalities were buried at sea. The six bodies were disinterred in 1913 and placed in a crypt below Perry's Victory and International Peace Memorial. The green park overlooks the busy harbor, the landing place of ferries from Middle Bass Island and Port Clinton.

After passing through the downtown area, the road reaches Perry's Victory and International Peace Memorial. The 25-acre park sits astride a narrow neck connecting the main bulk of South Bass with the smaller eastern portion. The isthmus was a marsh that was filled before construction of the memorial could begin in 1912. The Doric column was designed by Joseph Freedlander. It rises 352 feet above the lake and is built of pink granite topped with an 11-ton bronze urn. An elevator takes visitors to an open-air observation deck at the 317-foot level. Views from the platform extend to all the Erie Islands and overlook the battle site about 10 miles to the northwest in the vicinity of Middle Sister Island. The memorial took three years to complete and became a unit of the National Park Service in 1936. It is open May through October.

Go back along OH 357 and continue straight past Catawba Road. The sidewalk ends beyond the Miller Boat Line office, but there is room to walk on the shoulder as the road curves around the bay. Reach Oak Point Picnic Area, also known as Oak Point State Park, on your right. The park offers outstanding views of Put-in-Bay (the water), Put-in-Bay (the village), the memorial, and Gibraltar Island, which shelters the bay from the open lake. A gravel reef, called Alligator Bar, extends across the bay from Oak Point to Gibraltar. The island is home to the Franz Theodore Stone Laboratory, Ohio State University's biological field station. Perry posted lookouts on Gibraltar in 1813.

Back on the road, pass over a small inlet on a short bridge. The water to the left is Terwilliger's Pond, a nature preserve noted for its diverse aquatic plants, fish, and birds, including a rookery of black-crowned night herons.

Turn right off the highway past a wooden Ohio State building (a university bookstore is in the basement) and come to the brick Put-in-Bay Fish Hatchery (circa 1916). The state closed the hatchery in 1991 and converted it to a demonstration center. It is now open to the public and features exhibits and tanks of live fish. Continue along the street toward Peach Point, then follow the road as it hairpins to the left rear. Walk along the shoulder of West Shore Boulevard.

Opposite Mitchell Road (the second road to your left) is the Reidling Beach Runway, used in winter as an access ramp to the lake for vehicles and ice-fishing shanties. Where West Shore Boulevard curves left, a lane leads right into a Put-in-Bay Township park on the shore. After the curve, take the first dirt lane to your right. The track leads through a forest of sugar maple, ash, and hackberry. Keep straight to a T-intersection and turn left on Niagara Road.

The way climbs gradually to reach the island's highest point— 638 feet (about 70 feet above Lake Erie). Lands of South Bass Island State Park are on the right. Reach a T-intersection with Catawba Road and turn right. Crown Hill Cemetery, the island's oldest burial ground, is on your right at the corner. Some of the 19th-century tombstones are inscribed in German, a heritage from some of the early German winemaking families who immigrated to South Bass.

Very shortly turn left on Meechen Road. Go to the first intersection and turn right on Put-in-Bay Road. Follow this road back to Langram Road, turn right, and reach Lime Kiln Dock.

# East Harbor
# State Park
## Around the beaches and
## marshes of Lake Erie

*Hiking distance: 7½ miles*
*Hiking time: 4 hours*
*Map: USGS Gypsum*

**T**u-shu-way is the name the Erie called the big lake that now bears their name. It was the last of the Great Lakes to be discovered by white explorers, not appearing on maps of the New World until 1650. Father René de Bréhant de Galinée, a Sulpician priest, made a trip along the north shore in 1669 and called the area the "earthly paradise of Canada." John Melish, traveling in Ohio in 1810, came to view "the lake in all its glory." When reaching the shore, he was struck by the "beautiful, blue, placid surface." "The scenery [was] very picturesque," he wrote, "the view was really sublime. I was delighted in it."

By the mid-20th century, life along the lake bore little resemblance to that enjoyed by Native Americans and pioneers. Professor Elliot J. Tramer noted that "No . . . lake anywhere in the world has experienced such extensive changes as Lake Erie in the past 150 years." Throughout the decades of timbering, agricultural clearing, industrial development, and population growth, Lake Erie had been used as the dumping place for the wastes and by-products of millions of people.

Lake Erie was the first Great Lake to be affected overall by pollution. Sewage, industrial toxins, farm wastes, fertilizers that cause oxygen depletion, pesticides, detergents, and burgeoning trash all took their toll. Marshes around the lake were drained or filled. Aquatic plants declined greatly. Exotic species (139 alien species have been recorded since the 1800s) gained footholds and took over entire

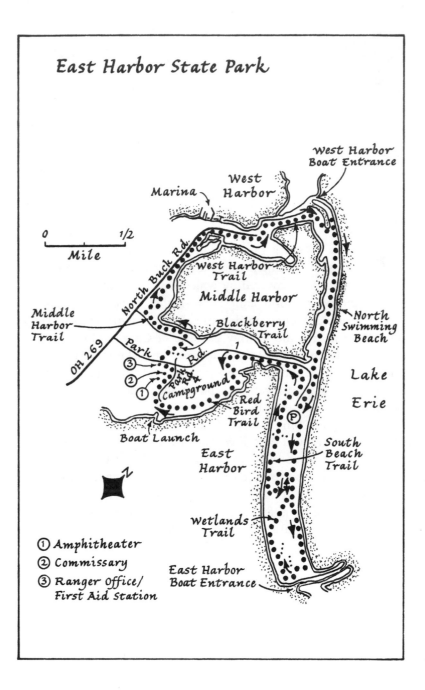

East Harbor State Park

West Harbor Boat Entrance

West Harbor

Marina

North Buck Rd.

West Harbor Trail

Middle Harbor

0    1/2
Mile

Middle Harbor Trail

OH 269

Park Rd.

Blackberry Trail

North Swimming Beach

Lake Erie

③
②
①
Ford Rd.
Campground

Red Bird Trail

P

Boat Launch

East Harbor

South Beach Trail

Wetlands Trail

East Harbor Boat Entrance

① Amphitheater
② Commissary
③ Ranger Office/
   First Aid Station

ecosystems. Competition from introduced species and overfishing caused the extinction of some species of fish and lowered the population levels of other species so that they were no longer able to reproduce. Some aquatic insects, especially those that depend on oxygenated water and serve as the base of the sport fish food chain, disappeared. Many of the recreational beaches along the lake were closed because of high bacterial counts from sewage discharges or were covered with dead fish and mats of decaying algae. By 1965 the great fishing industry of Lake Erie was no more, and the lake itself was pronounced "dead." Of course, it was not biologically dead. There was probably more life in the water than before, but it was life that was remarkably nondiverse (or less desirable from a human standpoint), composed of a relatively few species that could thrive in polluted, deoxygenated waters.

During the late 1960s remedial actions were planned, and by the early 1980s the first signs of lake recovery were observed. The extent of algal blooms was reduced. Dissolved oxygen levels increased. The concentration of dissolved solids decreased. Today the lake is once more a valued resource. Water-based recreation is a multibillion-dollar industry and the production of prized fish species (such as walleye) is at a record high. In 1995, the US Geological Survey reported that Lake Erie "is widely considered to be the best walleye fishery in the world."

Although some people now rank Lake Erie as the cleanest of the Great Lakes, it still faces many problems. A few beaches close each summer due to bacterial contamination. Exotic species continue to displace native plants and animals in what seems to be a never-ending downward spiral. The future of some fish such as sturgeon and some aquatic insects such as mayflies remains uncertain. All Lake Erie sport fish are safe to eat, but the Ohio Department of Health recommends that some fish consumption be restricted—just one walleye a week, for example. Erie's health now depends on how we treat this once pristine lake.

This hike circles East Harbor State Park, the largest Ohio state park on Lake Erie. You will see sandy beaches, teeming lagoons (East, Middle, and West Harbors), lush wetlands, verdant forests, and efforts to recover some of the lost biological diversity of the marshes. You will also find exotic species and human-made alterations to the waterfront, and witness some of the strain that approximately 17 million people who live in Lake Erie's drainage basin (about 40 percent of the total population of the Great Lakes basin) bring to bear on the lake.

## Access

East Harbor State Park lies at the end of OH 269. Turn right onto the main entrance road (Park Road 1), and drive to the beach. Turn right and park at the end of the big parking area.

## Trail

Walk along the gravel lane that runs off the parking area. The road once led to a swimming beach that was destroyed by storms and high water. Much of the beach was washed away and the lake now laps at the huge concrete blocks that serve to protect the shore from further erosion. Overgrown parking lots and abandoned buildings can be seen along the lane. At the second structure, the broad Wetlands Trail goes right through the trees. You will return to this spot later, but for now keep straight on the road. At the third structure, angle toward Lake Erie and walk along a wide, sandy beach. Kelleys and South Bass Islands are visible across the water.

You walk at the edge of the world's largest freshwater system—the Great Lakes. Lake Erie ranks fourth in size among the five Great Lakes (after Superior, Huron, and Michigan) and is the 12th largest lake on earth. It is 240 miles long by 30 to 58 miles wide. At 9940 square miles, it is larger than Vermont. Lake Erie now supports the largest fishery in the Great Lakes, yielding more fish than the other four Great Lakes combined. Ohio commercial fishermen harvested 5.3 million pounds of fish from Lake Erie in 1992. The combined fish catch (commercial and sporting) for the entire lake is an estimated 50–60 million pounds per year.

The beach will likely be littered with the small shells of zebra mussel, one of the latest exotic species to invade Lake Erie, appearing here in the late 1980s. This Eurasian species is thought to have been discharged with ballast water from foreign ships sailing to Great

*Dead shoreline trees are testimony to the force of Lake Erie's waves and winds.*

Lakes ports. The effect of zebra mussels on the lake's overall ecosystem is not yet clear, but they have severely reduced native mussels and may eventually eliminate them.

Just before reaching the East Harbor Boat Entrance (an inlet marked by long jetties of riprap), turn away from the lake toward a double row of sand fences. Make your way around the fences and pick up an open trail through the dunes and dune forest. Come to a T-junction and turn left on the Wetlands Trail. The Wetlands Trail is well named: Parts of it remain wet most of the year. Snowmobiles use this route when the ground is frozen. Reach the riprap wall lining the boat entrance and turn right along the channel. The trail curves right, away from the boat entrance, and leads through a forest of tall cottonwoods with a dense understory.

Fork left sharply. The trail comes close to marshy East Harbor, then angles onto an old asphalt road to come back to the gravel lane. Walk back along the lane to the broad entrance to the Wetlands Trail opposite the abandoned structure and turn left to enter the forest. Shortly reach a T-intersection and turn left. The way soon curves right and enters a long straightaway, the South Beach Trail. Ignore a few side trails that go right and left, until you come to a cross trail. Here a short walk to your left leads to a viewpoint overlooking East Harbor.

East Harbor is the first lagoon on your walk, an embayment behind the front dune that is a combination of open water and plant-choked wetland. Most of Lake Erie's back lagoons and marshes have been drained for agriculture or filled for other purposes. Shoreline stabilization and exotic species have altered the environment of others to such an extent that native wetland plants have been all but extirpated. The Ohio Department of Natural Resources is restoring marshland at East Harbor State Park by reestablishing native species and eliminating exotics such as common reed and purple loosestrife. The project shows good results. After two years, the number of species increased 53 percent, from 68 to 104, including nine state-listed rare plants. Many of the reestablished species had not been recorded at East Harbor State Park for nearly 30 years.

Return to the main trail and turn left to continue. Come upon a broad trail to your right and follow it to a grassy picnic area.

Turn left through the picnic area and shortly pick up a narrow paved bicycle trail that curves left to run along Park Road 1. East Harbor lies on your left and Middle Harbor can be seen across the road on your right. Follow the paved trail to a picnic area with shelter house on your left. The bicycle trail turns into the parking lot; walk through the lot and through an opening in the campground fence on the far side, keeping the latrines on your left. The way leads between campsites 104A and 105A and reaches a campground road; turn left.

The East Harbor campground, with 570 sites, is the largest in any Ohio state park. Beyond campsite 116A, turn left on the Red Bird Trail through a field. The trail soon reaches the shore of East Harbor and curves right. The path runs along a dike that separates open water on your left from a marsh on your right. Pass trails dropping down to the marsh and stay on the Red Bird Trail to the boat-launch area. Walk through the parking lot and follow Park Road 4.

Pass Park Road 9, the amphitheater, and the commissary on your left. Turn left on one-way Park Road 1, which leads to the ranger office/first aid station. Near the office turn right across Park Road 1 and enter a scrubby forest on the Blackberry Trail. Pass a side trail to your right and walk through a grove of white pines into a mowed field. Angle right at about the 2 o'clock position across the grass to reach a small parking lot and picnic area on the other side of a paved road.

The Middle Harbor Trail begins amid gigantic white oaks at the end of the parking lot. The trail quickly reaches the shore of Middle Harbor and turns left. The shallow, still waters of the lagoon abound with plants and animals engaged in unceasing activity and constant change. Middle Harbor is a wildlife sanctuary and the most natural of the lagoons in the park.

Come out of the woods at a T-intersection and turn right. Turn right again on the first side trail to walk through an upland forest of hickory and cherry. Come to another T-intersection and turn left. The path winds to reach a broad trail where you turn right, then soon turn right again on an even wider trail. The way shortly comes out onto North Buck Road; turn right and walk along the wide, grassy shoulder.

North Buck Road curves right at the East Harbor State Park Marina. Follow the road to the end and turn left on a gravel drive. The "No Trespassing/Private Drive" sign is meant to discourage vehicular traffic; hikers can use the drive to gain entry to the West Harbor Trail. Reach state land and a sign on a gate announcing the beginning of the trail. The way leads onto a graveled dike separating West Harbor (on your left) from marshy Middle Harbor (on your right). West Harbor is mostly lined with marinas and boat slips and is the most altered of the lagoons on today's walk. All of the waters in the park contain common carp, another Eurasian species, which was introduced to North America in 1831. Carp degrade shoaly waters such as the lagoons by causing excessive turbidity that can lead to declines in waterfowl and native fish. In May, you can see the water churning with carp as they spawn in the shallows along the West Harbor Trail.

The trail angles right when it reaches the channel leading out to the West Harbor Boat Entrance. Leave the dike behind and walk across sandy land clothed in forest with marsh on your right.

Come to a T-intersection among dunes and turn left to reach the small boat harbor at the entrance to West Harbor. A stone jetty leads from the strand out into Lake Erie. Walk along the jetty and pass through a zone of shrubs and reeds to get to the beach. Turn right and walk along the sandy shore.

The water before you is South Passage, seemingly wide and straight, but the channel is tortuous and shallow compared to Pelee Passage, which lies in Canadian waters between Pelee Island and Point Pelee. Thus, most of the big lake freighters take the northern passage. Twenty percent of the world's surface fresh water is in the Great Lakes, but only 4 percent of this amount is in Lake Erie, a function of its relative shallowness. The lake's shallowness has been both a curse and its salvation. The already rich waters responded quickly and strikingly to increased pollution. Yet Lake Erie's fast flushing time (water remains in the basin only about three years) assisted its dramatic response to cleanup of conventional pollution.

Soon reach North Swimming Beach. Four constructed offshore islands break the force of the waves and keep the beach safe for swimmers and help prevent erosion. Walk along the beach or through the picnic area behind it to return to your car.

# Resthaven
# Wildlife Area

## An indomitable prairie at the
## western edge of the Western Reserve

*Hiking distance: 3¼ miles*
*Hiking time: 2 hours*
*Maps: USGS Castalia; wildlife area map*

A vast wet marl prairie once wrapped around much of Sandusky Bay. Known to the early settlers as Castalia Prairie, the region is singularly different from the hardwood forests encountered in the rest of the Western Reserve. Historic accounts reported that the grass was so tall and thick that travel through the prairie was almost impossible. Farming, mining, and development chipped away over the years so that today little remains of the original prairie. Perhaps the best place to view the remnants is Resthaven Wildlife Area, which preserves about 2300 acres of restored prairie and scrub land on the site of an old marl pit.

In the early 20th century, the plentiful deposits of marl near the surface attracted miners who stripped away the calcarious clays to use in the manufacture of concrete. Their shallow slit trenches and chiseled spoil banks, now softened with dense thickets, can be seen along your walk.

Mining tapered off when marl was no longer used to produce cement. The state of Ohio began purchasing the strip lands in 1942 to establish an area for public hunting and fishing, but mining continued on other parts of the prairie until the late 1950s. Resthaven is noted for rabbit and pheasant hunting, while rails, snipe, woodcock, waterfowl, and a few gallinules also are bagged. The shallow marl excavation have filled with water and now are used by anglers going after largemouth bass, bluegill, crappies, northern pike, bullheads, and carp.

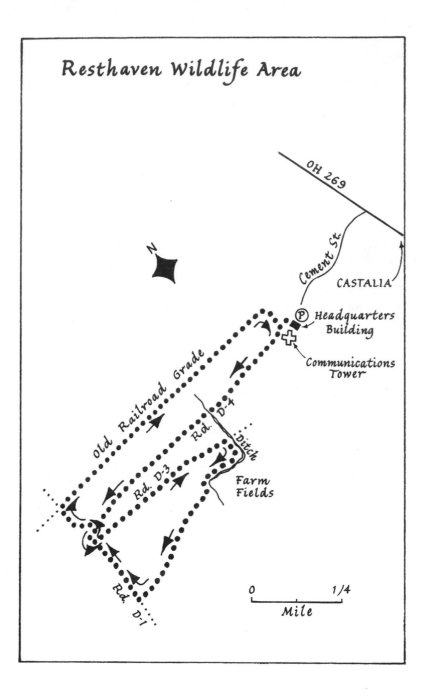

Resthaven Wildlife Area

The state primarily manages the area for game, but Resthaven ranks as a refuge for many other species rare in Ohio. The wildlife area is crowded with unusual plants, insects, and birds. Big bluestem, little bluestem, Indian grass, and prairie-dock can be found here. Resthaven supports one of the world's largest populations of small white lady's-slipper, a rare wild orchid. Also here is the closely related and equally uncommon small yellow lady's-slipper. These two species of orchids are known to hybridize when they grow close together. About 85 plants of this exceptionally rare hybrid have been recorded from Resthaven. The orchids bloom from the middle to the end of May.

With unusual plant communities come rare insects, especially butterflies and moths that depend on specific food plants to complete their life cycles. At least 14 species of uncommon moths have been collected at Resthaven, usually representing the easternmost populations in their ranges. Other than Castalia Prairie, most of these moths occur only in a few other prairie remnants in Illinois and Wisconsin.

That these rare and seemingly fragile species survived the long years of disturbance seems nothing short of miraculous. Six decades of mining with no reclamation irrevocably altered the landscape. Cutting, filling, and changing drainage patterns severely disrupted the prairie environment. Yet tenuous populations of moths, orchids, and grasses hung on, like embers from a dying campfire. Technology changed before they were completely extinguished. Now the prairie-loving plants and insects are considered small touchstones of a once wild continent. They abide at Resthaven under the protection of the state.

The wildlife area is also well known as a prime place to view the spring warbler migration. The diversified plant communities, consisting of grassland, prairie, woods, marsh, and low shrubs, bring the area alive with warblers of every kind. From late April to mid-May is the best time to see the migrating songbirds.

Your walk mostly follows interior access roads, dirt tracks, and an old railroad grade. The roads are open to vehicles in the warm months, but they are closed to all traffic from the beginning of upland game season in the fall until after the spring thaw. Call the wildlife area at 419-684-5049 for specific dates and other information.

## Access

Resthaven Wildlife Area is on the northwest edge of Castalia, a village noted for its artesian springs. From the center of town, go north on OH 269 for 0.3 mile. Turn left (west) onto Cement Street, which dead-ends at the wildlife area after 0.4 mile. Park near the headquarters building.

## Trail

Keep the headquarters, outbuildings, and communications tower on your left as you walk west along paved road D-4. The pavement ends beyond the tower; continue on a broad marl road, passing a gate locked in season. Wet prairie all around supports cattails, reeds, grasses, and scrubby trees such as willows, cottonwoods, ash, and elms. Cross a ditch and continue straight on the road.

After about ¾ mile, come to a major intersection. You will return to this spot later, but for now fork left and keep following the road to your left in a broad U as it turns east. A large marsh opens on your right. Follow the gravel road (D-3) to the end and then continue straight on a two-track lane. At the first ditch, turn right on a narrower lane, keeping the ditch on your left.

Shortly you will reach the boundary of the wildlife area, as indicated by farm fields to your front. Your way curves right, still with the ditch on your left, and follows the perimeter of state land on a ribbon of hard dirt.

Follow the lane as it curves to your left and then straightens to your right. This area is a good place to look on the trailway for pieces of marl—a pitted, light, spongelike, whitish rock. Reach a small, elongated pond on your left, while on your right is a series of long, water-filled trenches interspersed with low, rocky ridges. Soon the channels and mounds surround you, remains of the old marl mine that once covered Resthaven. Shrubby thickets of red-osier dogwood, distinguished by its bright red stems, choke the depressions, while poverty grass grows on the threadbare soil of the ridges.

Your track comes out onto gravel road D-1; turn right. Ponds open up on both sides of the road. Look for muskrats, mallards, wood duck, ring-necked duck, and Canada goose on the water. Red-

*Resthaven Wildlife Area (Beverly J. Brown)*

winged blackbirds and great blue herons are often seen among the shore reeds. Come to the major intersection you encountered earlier and turn right. Immediately take the left fork (your entrance trail from headquarters), but continue to your left by making a sharp turn to the left rear. This road (still labeled D-1) passes through a gate, curves right, and heads north.

After the road straightens, you soon reach an old railroad grade. Turn right and follow the straight gradient for about ¾ mile. These are the former Norfolk and Western Railroad tracks, abandoned in the late 1970s. Snakes frequent the rocky trail and use the rough stones on the old bed to help shed their skins.

When you reach an impenetrable thicket on the grade, turn right and cross a low opening, heading straight for the communications tower. You soon come to the entrance trail (road D-4). Turn left to return to the headquarters complex where you parked your car.

# Sheldon Marsh
# State Nature Preserve

### An easy walk featuring superb wildlife habitats and luxuriant wildflowers

*Hiking distance: 1½ miles*
*Hiking time: 1 hour*
*Maps: USGS Huron; preserve map*

Sheldon Marsh on the shore of Lake Erie was well known for its excellent waterfowl hunting before it was set aside as a state nature preserve. It has since gained fame among birders as one of the best sites in the Midwest for observing spring and fall migrants. The preserve's location near the intersection of the Atlantic and Mississippi flyways makes it ideal for multitudes of birds that need to rest and feed either before or after the long flight over the lake. Some 300 species have been sighted year-round, about one-third of all bird species in the United States.

The extraordinary richness of the avian fauna depends on the diverse habitats found on the preserve. The 387-acre refuge includes flowered meadows, old fields, scrub thickets, closed-canopy forests, vernal pools, a pond, swamps, marshes, lagoons, mud flats, barrier beaches, and the open waters of Lake Erie.

Tundra swans drop in during their migration between their nesting grounds in the arctic and their overwintering areas on Chesapeake Bay. Dabbling ducks are common in the marshes. Diving ducks—often numbering in the thousands—can be seen on Lake Erie. Look for a wide variety of shorebirds on the mud flats. The forests and thickets harbor many warblers, vireos, flycatchers, kinglets, and other small songbirds. Bald eagles, ospreys, and 11 different kinds of hawks are often visible high in the trees or soaring over open areas. Nesting birds on the preserve include species as diverse as prothonotary warblers and Cooper's hawks.

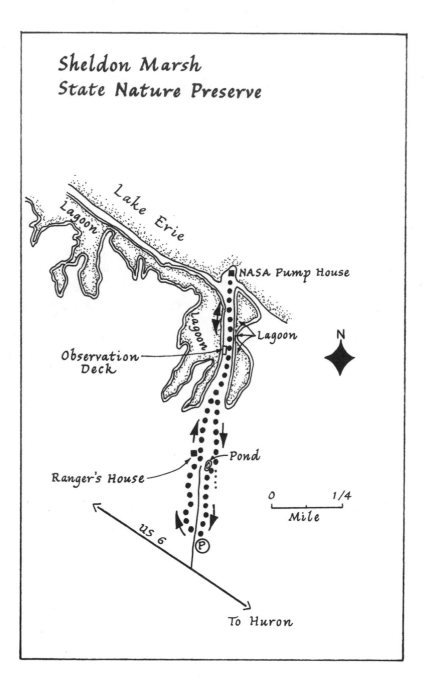

With the birds are found many other animals. Your trail affords one of the best places in the state to observe muskrats. Whitetail deer, raccoon, eastern chipmunk, eastern fox squirrel, and many smaller mammals can be seen by the quiet hiker. The preserve protects habitat for two reptiles rare in Ohio—eastern fox snake and Blanding's turtle. Frogs are abundant in the wetlands and salamanders live under rocks and logs in the forest. Management activities also help establish resting and feeding areas for monarch butterflies during their migrations.

The mature hardwood forests on the property have been spared from grazing and wholesale logging. As a result, a remarkable display of delicate woodland wildflowers are enjoyed by hikers each spring. Trilliums, jack-in-the-pulpit, wild geranium, trout lily, wild ginger, Dutchman's breeches, violets, toothworts, May-apple, and orchids thrust through the rich humus under the tall trees. In wet areas, marsh-marigold in spring and cardinal flower in summer are spectacularly vibrant. The meadows and fields are colored in late summer and fall with goldenrods, clovers, and asters.

The property has changed little since the early 1950s, when Dean Sheldon of Sandusky acquired title and began long-range conservation practices to restore and enhance wildlife habitat. The elaborate gate at the entrance along US 6 retains the old spelling—Sheldon's Marsh. The state established the nature preserve in 1979.

A paved service road runs the length of the preserve from the parking lot to near Lake Erie. This road and an adjoining observation platform at the marsh are wheelchair-accessible. Benches along the way provide spots for resting or wildlife watching. Your walk wanders on and off the pavement to explore as many paths as possible. The unpaved portions of the trail can be very muddy, especially in spring. Preserve regulations require you to stay on the service road or trails; dogs are prohibited.

## Access

From downtown Huron, go west on US 6 for 2.6 miles. Watch carefully for the entrance to the preserve on your right. You must make a sharp right turn off a high-speed, busy highway through a narrow gate.

*Sheldon Marsh State Nature Preserve (Beverly J. Brown)*

## Trail

From the parking lot, walk along the paved service road, pass the bulletin board on your left, and soon turn left on a path through a dense thicket. This trail is usually very muddy during wet seasons; you can continue straight on the pavement as an alternate way and rejoin the hike down the road.

The path winds through thickset brush of white pine, red maple, silver maple, honey locust, and multiflora rose. The trail eventually angles back to the paved road. Turn left onto the asphalt and enter a mature forest of towering trees and open understory. You are walking along the original road to Cedar Point Amusement Park in Sandusky. The entrance drive was built around the turn of the century but abandoned in the 1930s after waves repeatedly washed out the pavement along the beach. A new road was built farther to the west.

Walk past a ranger's house on your left and soon come out of the woods. The marsh opens on your left. Another paved road comes in from the right rear; this is your return loop, but for now continue straight. The way soon becomes bordered on both sides by marshlands and open water.

A low observation platform on the left provides outstanding views of the teeming marsh. There is much to see and absorb here. Few areas along Lake Erie remain as wild and free as Sheldon Marsh. The verdant wetlands, moss-blanketed forests, and unspoiled barrier beaches move to the immemorial rhythms of winter ice, spring and fall migration, and summer plenty. Watch for muskrats swimming through the murky water, often carrying sprigs of aquatic vegetation back to their lodges. Scan the far shore for great egrets, motionless in the shallows as they wait for a passing fish or frog. Ring-billed gulls keen overhead and turkey vultures wheel in graceful arcs. The quacks and honks of ducks and geese may be the most noticeable sound, but listen for the more distant song of small birds in the trees. Sometimes you can hear the wind rattling the leaves of the cottonwoods that line the lake shore. On warm spring days, you may catch pungent, rich whiffs of the swamp mixed with the wonderful smell of the earth.

Walk on down the road to the end, where you will see a concrete building surrounded by a high fence. This facility is a pump house used by NASA to draw water from the lake for its Plum Brook Station, about 5 miles inland to the southwest. The building sits at the east end of the Cedar Point sand spit, a 7-mile-long barrier strand that ends at the amusement park. The beach around the NASA site has been stabilized, but over a mile of undeveloped beaches are left in their natural state west of the building. They are dynamic land forms and are geologically very active, retreating landward into the marsh because of recent high-water periods on the lake.

Turn and walk back along the service road. Fork left when you reach the other paved road. Continue to the Old-Field Trail and turn right. Follow the path to the left around an artificial pond, built in the 1950s by Sheldon.

The trail leads back to the parking area through a meadow maintained by the Firelands Audubon Society as a haven for butterflies. The field attracts hundreds of migrating monarchs as they stop to feed on red and white clover during their autumn journey to Mexico and Central America. Mid-September is usually the best time to see them at Sheldon Marsh.

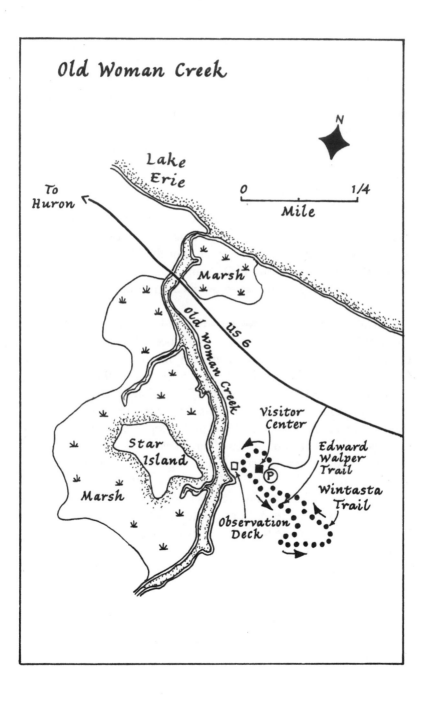

# Old Woman Creek

## Easy walking along a superlative estuary of international significance

*Hiking distance: 1 mile*
*Hiking time: ½ hour*
*Maps: USGS Huron; preserve map*

At first glimpse, Old Woman Creek seems unremarkable, just one of many minor streams that flow directly into Lake Erie. The creek carves a crooked 10-mile trek through a bountiful agricultural basin of barely 30 square miles. Travelers on US 6 cross the creek on the short bridge near its mouth but rarely cast a sideways glance; no sign announces its name.

But a closer look reveals that Old Woman Creek is unique. It is one of Ohio's and the Great Lakes' best remaining examples of a natural estuary. Estuaries are traditionally defined as bodies of water where fresh water meets and mixes with the salt water of the sea and where water levels are affected by tides. The result is an intermediate environment, a place that is very different from both freshwater and saltwater habitats. Lake Erie is, of course, not a saltwater sea, and there is no give and pull of the tides on its shores. Yet the waters of the creek and the lake combine in the estuary to form a distinctive aquatic environment, one that is chemically different from that of either the creek or the lake. Water levels in the estuary also fluctuate, not because of tides, but because of storms, winds, and other weather conditions.

Estuaries are noted for their extraordinary richness and diversity of life. They straddle an ecological boundary between river and lake, between land and aquatic systems. Scientists have found them to be among the most productive natural places on earth. Climate and location make Old Woman Creek home to a stunningly rich and varied

*The observation deck on the Edward Walper Trail (Beverly J. Brown)*

flora and fauna, ranging from microscopic diatoms and zooplankton, through vascular plants such as American water lotus, to top-of-the-food-chain predators like eastern fox snake and bald eagle.

The exceptional features of Old Woman Creek are recognized by the state, which set aside a 571-acre nature preserve, and by the National Oceanic and Atmospheric Administration, which designated the preserve as one of 22 national research reserves in the country. Old Woman Creek is the only freshwater reserve in the National

Estuarine Reserve Research System and the only one on the Great Lakes. Estuaries like Old Woman Creek are now considered uncommon, since all of the big rivers and most of the creeks that flow into the lake have been channelized, polluted, dredged, or otherwise altered.

The visitor center near the trailhead features interesting exhibits and displays on the early inhabitants, natural history, and European settlement of the area. The center helps meet one of the main goals of the preserve—to educate the public on how the waters of creeks and estuaries are inseparable from the life and quality of Lake Erie and why it is important to protect wild areas like Old Woman Creek. A stop at the visitor center before your walk will help you understand the history and ecology of the estuary, including the intricate life patterns of its plant and animal communities and the ecological balances that sustain them.

Another major goal of the preserve—research—is provided by the Ohio Center for Coastal Wetlands Studies, housed in the visitor center and in buildings on the lake shore. Scientists and students use the sanctuary as a natural field station to study the complex ecological relationships occurring in estuarine systems.

Your walk begins on the Edward Walper Trail, but after ¼ mile it switches to the Wintasta Trail to explore the more remote areas of the reserve. The Edward Walper Trail honors the farmer who sold his land to the state in 1978.

The Wintasta Trail is named for a Huron woman who legend says was killed trying to save her lover, a French trader, from execution. Minehonto, the mother of Wintasta, was so overcome with grief that she drowned herself in the creek the night after Wintasta's death. White settlers who later heard the story named the creek "Old Woman."

The nature preserve is open to the public from April to December. It is closed on weekends from January to March, but the offices and visitor center are open most weekdays. The visitor center is closed Mondays and Tuesdays throughout the year. The center and the first 810 feet of trail are accessible to people in wheelchairs. The path is paved to the observation deck overlooking the widest portion of the estuary. Dogs are not allowed on the trails. I recommend hiking boots for this short walk because of the frequent muddy conditions encountered beyond the pavement.

## Access

From the junction of US 6 and OH 13 in downtown Huron, head east on US 6. Drive 2.7 miles and turn right onto the entrance road for Old Woman Creek State Nature Preserve and National Estuarine Research Reserve. Reach the parking lot in another 0.2 mile and leave your car near the visitor center.

## Trail

The blacktop Edward Walper Trail leaves the parking area to the right of the visitor center. Wind through open fields and young woods to an observation deck on the eastern shore of the estuary. The wide, still waters of the creek resemble a pond. In the middle sits Star Island, now thickly forested but the site of a vineyard in the late 1800s. Wild grapes now thrive in the area as evidenced by the many vines hanging from trees along the path.

The little estuary opens to the vast lake less than ½ mile downstream. Here you are standing near the southernmost point on the southernmost lake in the Great Lakes. Nipigon Bay on Lake Superior's upper shore lies 600 miles to the northwest. To the northeast, Lake Ontario sends all of the Great Lakes' water past Wolfe Island into the St. Lawrence River, almost 400 miles from Old Woman Creek.

The trail is graveled beyond the deck and stays close to the water. After leaving the creek, the path forks. The left fork leads to the visitor center. Here you keep right on the Wintasta Trail and step onto a boardwalk through a bottomland hardwood forest. The way climbs, then descends again into the bottom and crosses it on another boardwalk. Beyond this point, the trail is not covered with gravel and can be quite muddy in places, especially in spring.

Your path stays mainly in the oak-hickory woods but occasionally passes through scrubby fields and thickets. Eastern bluebird boxes in the old fields were set up by the state. Bluebirds may appear as early as the first week of March to inspect the houses and establish breeding territories.

Boardwalks lift the trail above lowland mire and woodland seeps, but you will still encounter many wet areas. As you approach the visitor center and parking lot, the Edward Walper Trail comes in from the left. Keep straight and return to your car.

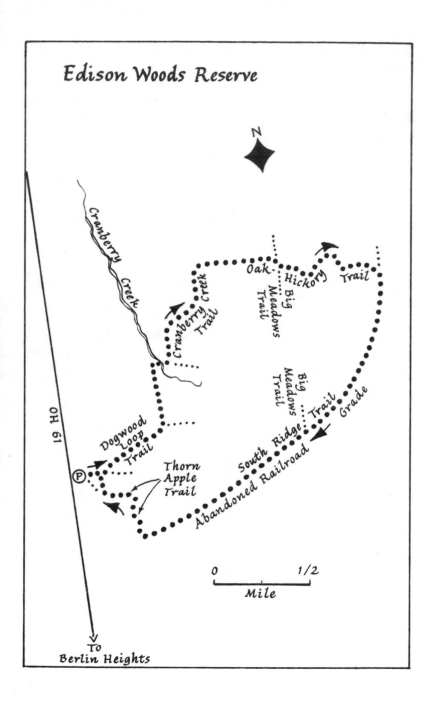

# Edison Woods Reserve

N

Cranberry Creek

Cranberry Creek Trail

Oak

Hickory Trail

Big Meadows Trail

Big Meadows Trail

OH 61

Dogwood Loop Trail

P

Thorn Apple Trail

South Ridge Trail Grade

Abandoned Railroad

0        1/2
Mile

To Berlin Heights

# Edison Woods Reserve

### A loop trail through lowland and upland forests

*Hiking distance: 5 miles*
*Hiking time: 2½ hours*
*Map: USGS Berlin Heights*

Edison Woods Reserve protects almost 1400 acres of forest. Erie MetroParks maintains the land in a natural, unaltered state. Except for two small parking lots and a few picnic tables at the entrance, the only development has been a network of trails for hikers and horses. The park is a good place to go to enjoy wild plants and animals.

The Western Reserve lies in the vast deciduous forest region of eastern North America. In a relatively undisturbed forest such as Edison Woods, about 35 percent of the plant species are broad-leaved trees and shrubs. Sixty percent are perennial herbs, and approximately 5 percent are annuals that complete their life cycles in one season. Upwards of 2000 species of plants are found in the Western Reserve.

The abundance and variety of hardwood trees at Edison Woods combine with a perfect climate to produce a remarkable fall foliage display. Each autumn, the leaves become brightly colored just before falling, painting the forest in a patchwork of reds, yellows, oranges, and browns. Conditions vary depending on the weather, but the height of color for Edison Woods is usually from the middle to the end of October. The completed cycle takes about three weeks and peak color lasts about a week.

## Access

Edison Woods Reserve is in Berlin Township. From the center of Berlin Heights, drive north 1.1 miles on OH 61. Turn right into the small gravel parking lot near the highway.

## Trail

Your wood-chipped path, the Dogwood Loop Trail, begins at the rear of the parking area. It and other trails in the park become waterlogged during wet seasons. Some of the trails are also used by horses, so expect churned up, muddy conditions in places. Waterproof boots are recommended.

The Dogwood Loop Trail curves onto a lane. Follow the lane, which is paralleled on the right beyond a hedgerow by a gravel road that leads to the horseman's parking area. Just after the road curves right to the parking area, a side trail enters from the right. You will return to this spot later, but for now keep straight on the broad lane.

Fork left off the lane and follow a wide path through the dense forest. Farther along, take the first trail to your left, leaving the Dogwood Loop Trail and walking along a connecting trail that leads through wet woods. Pin oak, swamp white oak, green ash, and American elm are the dominant trees.

The path eventually enters a drier forest, where upland species such as white oak, red oak, shagbark hickory, flowering dogwood, and basswood grow. The way turns right at a 90-degree angle onto an old roadway (the former Deehr Road). Very soon the trail dips slightly to cross the headwaters of Cranberry Creek, a short stream that arises in the park and flows north into Lake Erie at Ruggles Beach. Just after you climb out of the shallow creek bed, turn left on the Cranberry Creek Trail; the Deehr Road Trail continues straight here.

The Cranberry Creek Trail curves through the woods to come out upon an electric utility right-of-way. Turn right and follow the wide, straight Oak-Hickory Trail under the wires. Reach a T-intersection with the Big Meadows Trail. Turn right, walk a short distance along this broad trail, then turn left on a narrow footpath, the continuing Oak-Hickory Trail. This stretch tends to be very wet at times.

The meandering Oak-Hickory Trail ends as it climbs a short, steep bank to reach the South Ridge Trail; turn right. The wide South Ridge Trail follows an abandoned railroad grade along the north face of a long, sandstone ridge. The way passes through an upland forest of bur oak, sugar maple, basswood, and American beech. Each spring, the vivid display of large-flowered or white trillium on the north-

*Large-flowered trillium grows in profusion at Edison Woods Reserve.*

facing slope is magnificent. The peak blooming time is between April and June.

Pass the Big Meadows Trail as it drops off the ridge to the right. Farther along, angle right on the Thorn Apple Trail as it descends the slope. The old railroad grade is blocked by fallen logs and branches at this spot. Switchback down the ridge. After the trail levels, you arrive in the vicinity of the horseman's parking area. Before reaching the opening, turn right on a short footpath that leads to the Dogwood Loop Trail. Turn left and follow the path back to your car.

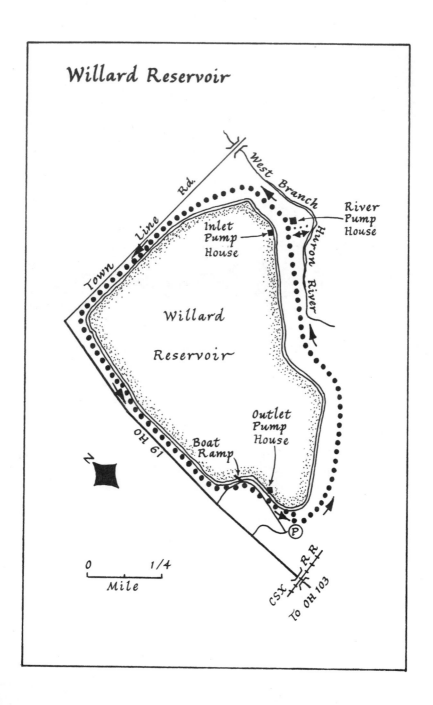

Willard Reservoir

# Willard Reservoir

## Around an upground reservoir

*Hiking distance: 2½ miles*
*Hiking time: 1 hour*
*Map: USGS Willard*

Willard Reservoir is an upground reservoir, an earthen structure designed by civil engineers to impound water in an upland location. Upground reservoirs are located off the main channels of streams, so that water has to be pumped uphill to fill them. A low head dam or other impounding structure on a nearby creek or river is necessary to provide the water depth required to submerge the pump intake. Willard Reservoir gets its water from the West Branch of the Huron River.

Upground reservoirs are unique in that you have to climb steeply to get to them. They are the closest thing to crater lakes to be found in the Western Reserve. Their unusual design sometimes leads to problems. Willard Reservoir leaked so much when it was built in 1971 that it had to be drained and repaired. The reservoir stores drinking water for the city of Willard.

Prior to construction of the storage reservoir, Willard obtained its water from deep wells that supplied about 1.2 million gallons a day. Willard's population of 5900 used about 1.1 million gallons a day in 1965, so there was an urgent need to find new sources of fresh water. The Northwest Ohio Water Development Plan, an initiative of the Ohio Department of Natural Resources, recommended construction of an upground storage reservoir. Willard was given the highest priority of some 36 new upground reservoirs proposed by the plan. Taken piecemeal, the small reservoirs and low dams built under the plan were minor compared to other bigger and better-known water development projects elsewhere in the country. But collectively the plan touched every major river in Northwest Ohio and forever changed the landscape. The immensity of the project is most readily seen from the air, where, in addition to the short, silvery threads of free-flowing rivers, you can see a huge, intricate system of reservoirs glittering in the sun, a picture in which the natural force of water has been changed by the force of human determination into a remarkably different structure.

The plan stated, "The upground reservoir is particularly adaptable to the relatively flat topography of Northwest Ohio, and offers an extremely flexible and economical means of developing the area's inland surface water supply." Demand for fresh water, whether pumped from wells or lakes or diverted from rivers, sends the Western Reserve's growing communities on a search that never ends. The plan concluded, "This reservoir will assure Willard . . . public water supplies for the 40-year period"—that is, until about 2011.

Although providing drinking water was the main purpose of the Water Development Plan, it was recognized that the new reservoirs could "offer great potential for meeting the needs of water-oriented recreation" in an area of the state with fewer public lands than other regions. A substantial part of the plan is devoted to discussing possible recreational uses of upground reservoirs, especially fishing, boating, swimming, and hunting. Hiking can now be added to the list. Your walk circles the 215-acre reservoir in a counterclockwise direction, with a short side trail to explore the pump station and dam on the Huron. Most of the trail is in open country.

## Access

From the junction of OH 103 and US 224 in Willard, drive north on OH 103 (Main Street) to its end at OH 61 northeast of town. Turn left on OH 61. Go under the railroad tracks and turn right at the first opportunity into a paved parking lot at the base of a high levee. There is no sign at this entrance, which is only 0.3 mile from the junction of OH 61 and OH 103. Rest rooms and drinking water are available.

## Trail

Walk through the mowed grass area along the base of the reservoir levee, keeping it on your left. About 2.3 billion gallons of water sit on the other side of the earthen wall. The forest on your right is a

*View from the high dike at Willard Reservoir (Beverly J. Brown)*

mixture of upland and lowland areas, sometimes opening out into marshes and wet meadows.

The thick forest squeezes close to the levee and you are faced with a choice of scrambling across the steep slope or climbing to the level top along the shore. Come to the redbrick pump station on your right, connected to the West Branch by a channel. Follow the channel for a view of the Huron. A small dam just downstream of the channel helps to augment the water supply during periods of low flow. The reservoir contains fish species such as rock bass, green sunfish, carp, and suckers because they have been pumped from the river. The Ohio Division of Wildlife stocks additional fish in the reservoir for anglers: largemouth and smallmouth bass, bluegill, yellow perch, walleye, brown bullhead, and channel catfish. Stocking is done annually because the reservoir is uniformly deep and has limited shallow areas for the growth of bottom organisms that serve as the principal food source for game fish.

From the pump station, follow the two-track service road that leads through a locked gate to a parking area on Town Line Road. Climb the slope and continue on the flat top of the levee. Limestone riprap borders the shoreline. Fine views of the reservoir and the surrounding countryside are offered from the high dike. Follow the levee as it curves left. Walk past the boat ramp and the outlet pump house. Descend the long stairs to the parking lot.

# Norwalk Reservoirs

## A trio of reservoirs
## serving people and wildlife

*Hiking distance: 1½ miles*
*Hiking time: 1 hour*
*Map: USGS Norwalk*

This circuit hike weaves around the shores of three reservoirs, two of which were created in 1896 by damming Norwalk Creek. The reservoirs were engineered as a source of drinking water for the city of Norwalk. They also have become stopovers in spring and autumn for migrating flocks of ducks, geese, and grebes. Hawks patrol the fields and woodlands near the water and gulls wheel about overhead.

Norwalk Reservoirs are famed for their good fishing, a fact borne out by the numerous great blue herons stalking the shallows and the belted kingfishers diving into the water. Human anglers flock to the reservoirs to try for walleye, saugeye, large- and smallmouth bass, bluegill, white crappie, channel catfish, and bullheads. The Ohio Division of Wildlife stocks the waters annually.

The reservoirs are in the heart of the Firelands, a 500,000-acre tract in the westernmost reaches of the Western Reserve. The land was granted to the residents of several Connecticut towns in 1792. During the American Revolution, their property had been burned by British forces often led by the traitorous Benedict Arnold. Most of the attacks occurred on coastal communities in the late 1770s and the early 1780s, during the closing years of the war. The British were seeking vengeance on townsfolk grown wealthy from raiding His Majesty's ships. The Connecticut General Assembly, holding its rich western territory ready for postwar expansion, sought to compensate the state's citizens for their hardships. The Firelands or "Sufferers' Lands" were given to 1870 "sufferers" whose total losses exceeded $800,000.

Native rights had to be addressed before the whites could claim their new lands. Under the Treaty of Greene Ville (1795), Native

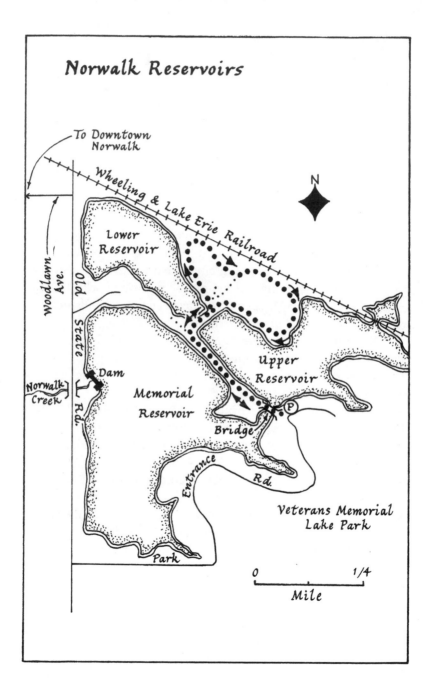

Norwalk Reservoirs

To Downtown
Norwalk

Wheeling & Lake Erie Railroad

N

Lower
Reservoir

Woodlawn
Ave.

Old
State
Rd.

Upper
Reservoir

Dam

Norwalk
Creek

Memorial
Reservoir

Bridge

P

Entrance
Rd.

Veterans Memorial
Lake Park

Park

0                    1/4
Mile

*The 49-acre Upper Reservoir is over 100 years old. (Beverly J. Brown)*

Americans retained all of Northwest Ohio west of the Cuyahoga River except for a few sites identified as strategic forts and major trading posts. A new treaty was negotiated with local chiefs of the Ottawa, Chippewa, Pottawatomie, Shawnee, Muncie, and Delaware tribes, "extinguishing aboriginal title" over 2.7 million acres of land in northern Ohio, including all of the Firelands and other areas of the Western Reserve west of the Cuyahoga. The ceremonies were conducted on July 4, 1805, at a small blockhouse called Fort Industry (now Toledo). Soon the surveyors laid out the townships and settlers began to move in. The Connecticut pioneers named many of their new settlements after their homeland: Norwalk (settled in 1809, 30 years after the British raid on Norwalk, Connecticut), Greenwich, Fairfield, Danbury, New Haven, East Haven, New London, Ridgefield, and Groton.

The Firelands encompass all of Huron County, most of Erie County, the Catawba Island and Marblehead Peninsulas in Ottawa County, and Ruggles Township in Ashland County.

Your walk is mostly through open areas surrounding the reservoirs. A forested section provides variety and opportunities to see woodland birds and mammals. The woods trails are frequently muddy and bordered by poison ivy.

## Access

The reservoirs are in Veterans Memorial Lake Park, a Norwalk city park. From downtown Norwalk, drive north on OH 61 (East Main Street). After about 0.2 mile, turn right on Woodlawn Avenue and drive for about 1 mile to a T-intersection with Old State Road. You are facing park land surrounding Norwalk Reservoirs at this point. Historic Woodlawn Cemetery (1854) is on your right. Turn right on Old State Road. Drive 0.8 mile, passing the first entrance to Veterans Memorial Lake Park on your left and crossing Norwalk Creek below a dam, and turn left into the second park entrance. Follow the paved park road for 0.8 mile as it curves around Memorial Reservoir (Reservoir 3) on your left. Park near the sign that reads "Norwalk Reservoir 2."

## Trail

Facing the sign, turn left and walk across the bridge between two reservoirs. A low spillway under the wide span carries water from Upper Reservoir (Reservoir 2) on your right to the larger Memorial Reservoir on your left. The 101-acre Memorial Reservoir was built in 1954 when it became apparent that Norwalk's drinking water needs were outgrowing the capacity of the two smaller reservoirs. The new reservoir more than doubled the size of water surface. The reservoir complex serves as Norwalk's only public water supply. If necessary, the city can supplement the supply by pumping water directly into Memorial Reservoir from the East Branch of the Huron River.

Continue along the dike, but at the first opportunity turn right on a high levee. The water far below on your left is Lower Reservoir (Reservoir 1). The way soon splits, with a trail descending to your left off the dike. Take this path down and enter a young woods. Turn left sharply where the trail ahead forks, and follow a broad trail that soon enters a plantation of old, tall pines and spruces.

Your way narrows and then enters a brushy area as it veers away from Lower Reservoir. The path curves right again and comes to a T-intersection at the bottom of a dike. Turn left and follow a woods road.

Come out into a grassy expanse. Railroad tracks are visible to your left. Walk straight across the meadow to the shore of Upper Reservoir and turn right. Follow the water's edge to return to the high levee and then retrace your steps to where you parked your car.

# Findley State Park

## A loop through forests and meadows

*Hiking distance: 3¼ miles*
*Hiking time: 2 hours*
*Maps: USGS Sullivan and Wellington;*
*park map; Buckeye Trail, Norwalk section*

The trails at Findley State Park traverse stately woodlands and feature picturesque views of Wellington Creek, a tributary of the West Branch of the Black River. Guy B. Findley, a Lorain County Common Pleas judge, purchased worn-out agricultural land in the 1930s and began forest management practices. He donated the land to the state of Ohio, and the park was established in 1950.

The forest now covers most of the land. Pines planted by the Civilian Conservation Corps can still be seen, but the mixed hardwoods native to this part of Ohio are reclaiming most of their habitat. In addition to red and white pine, trees along the trail include red maple, sugar maple, white ash, black cherry, basswood, American beech, and a variety of oaks and hickories. The forest also supports a wealth of woodland shrubs and wildflowers. Low, swampy clearings are especially rich with marsh marigold, cardinal flower, common buttonbush, and many obscure species, including a sedge known only by its Latin name, *Carex lacustris.*

The presence of *Carex lacustris,* found at Findley only in a 1000-square-foot isolated wetland, is noteworthy because this low-growing sedge is thought to be the only food plant in Ohio for the larvae of Duke's skipper, a butterfly considered among the rarest in the country. Like other scarce Ohio butterflies, such as the two-spotted skipper and the silver-bordered fritillary, Duke's skipper is a habitat specialist, not a generalist that can live in a variety of communities. Leland L. Martin, a local amateur entomologist, discovered Duke's

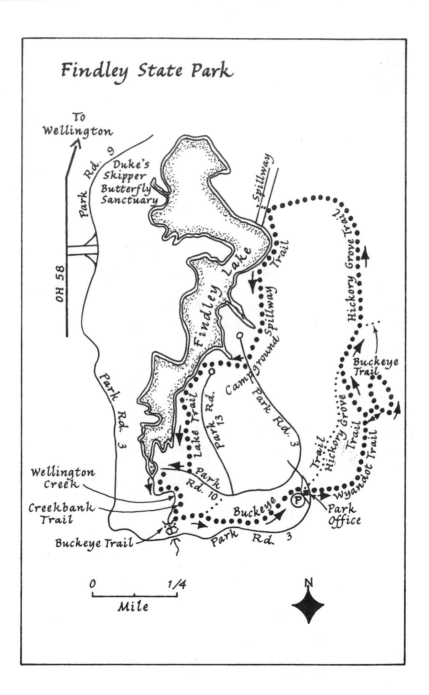

Findley State Park

To Wellington

Park Rd. 9

Duke's Skipper Butterfly Sanctuary

OH 58

Park Rd. 3

Findley Lake

Spillway

Spillway Trail

Hickory Grove Trail

Buckeye Trail

Campground Park Rd. 3

Lake Trail

Park Rd. 13

Trail Hickory Grove Trail

Wyandot Trail

Wellington Creek

Creekbank Trail

Buckeye Trail

Park Rd. 10

Buckeye

P

Park Office

Park Rd. 3

0        1/4
Mile

N

skipper in the park in 1972. In 1981, the Ohio Department of Natural Resources established the Duke's Skipper Butterfly Sanctuary, the first in the state. The sanctuary is in the northwest corner of the park, off Park Road 9.

Duke's skipper was formerly known only from Alabama and Virginia, so its occurrence in Ohio caused considerable interest in the scientific world. The skipper served as a model to explain how northern Ohio may have been repopulated by animals and plants after being completely denuded during the last glaciation. The range of Duke's skipper and some other species suggests an invasion route from the Gulf Coastal Plain up the Mississippi Valley to the Great Lakes region, possibly following the Wabash Valley. When the climate turned warmer and drier approximately 5000 years ago, many of the smaller wetlands along this route may have dried up, effectively isolating the Great Lakes populations from the parent populations in the South. This skipper has since been collected from several disjunct localities in Northwest Ohio, Indiana, and Michigan, thus lending support to the theory.

Duke's skipper remains uncommon, found only in isolated, specialized habitats where *Carex lacustris* grows—usually the wettest parts of sedge meadows. Both skipper and sedge are inconspicuous, two of what Professor Carolyn V. Platt calls "the humbler plants and animals that form the warp and weft of Ohio's fraying natural fabric." In northern Ohio, Duke's skipper produces only a single brood each year. Adults are on the wing in July. They are small (about 1½ inches long), dark, with a swift and darting flight. The reclusive caterpillars are believed to come out to feed only at night, spending their days hidden in nests, further decreasing the likelihood of spotting this rare skipper. But your chances of observing other species are good because Findley State Park abounds in insects of all kinds. Among butterflies, I have seen other skippers, as well as satyrs, fritillaries, coppers, blues, sulphurs, buckeye, monarch, mourning cloak, red spotted purple, and at least four different kinds of swallowtails along this trail. Fireflies glitter in the oak woods and crickets skirl from the undergrowth on midsummer evenings.

## Access

Findley State Park is about 2.3 miles south of Wellington off OH 58. Once inside the park, follow signs to the park office and campground. Pass through the camp check station and immediately turn left into the camp visitor parking area.

## Trail

Your circuit hike begins on the Wyandot Trail, a ½-mile self-guiding nature trail built and maintained by the Black River Audubon Society. Stop at the office and pick up a descriptive pamphlet keyed to the numbered stations along the way. The trail begins across the road from the office on a broad swath that soon narrows to a single-file footpath when it turns to enter the forest.

Oaks and hickories grow profusely here but later you pass through a beech–sugar maple forest. A few of the white oaks are remarkable for their height and girth. They were left when this land was cleared for agriculture and now they are surrounded by much smaller trees. Basswood is a common subdominant species. Poison ivy is prolific both on the ground and on tree trunks.

After station 13, turn right on a short loop trail that leads out of the forest and around an old field. Turn right when you reach the opening. The change in plant cover and the associated animal community is dramatic. Particularly imposing is the high wall of green presented by the summer trees as you walk back toward the forest from the meadow. Return to the main trail after the meadow loop and go right to continue the hike.

The Wyandot Trail ends at the junction with the Buckeye and the Hickory Grove Trails. Turn right. Where the Buckeye Trail goes right, continue straight on the Hickory Grove Trail. Walk for about ½ mile on a broad path through a second-growth forest. Come out of the woods into a great grassy clearing above the emergency spillway from Findley Lake. Wellington Creek was dammed in the mid-1950s to create the 93-acre lake, used by park visitors for swimming, boating, and fishing.

Do not descend off the levee. Rather, turn left and find your wide trail as it soon reenters the forest. You are now on the Spillway

*Beeches and maples abound in Findley State Park. (Beverly J. Brown)*

Trail following a utility line right-of-way on the high ground above the lake.

The Spillway Trail ends at the park's campground as it reaches Park Road 3 in the vicinity of campsite 88. Jog left, walk a short distance along the road, and then turn right at campsite 112 to pick up the narrow Lake Trail. A sign behind the campsite marks its beginning.

Your way descends and ascends steeply and then skirts the end of another campground road turnaround on your left. Shortly after the campground, keep left on a broad trail. The narrower spur leading straight here reaches a bluff overlooking Findley Lake.

Come out on Park Road 10. Turn right and go downhill past the park's material yard on your right and reach the boat-launch ramp. Turn left off the road onto the Creekbank Trail. This path meanders through the flats and across the floodplain adjacent to Wellington Creek. Cardinal flower adds its brilliant red blossoms to the lowlands in late summer. This bottom is mosquito-infested and can be very muddy in wet seasons.

Reach the Buckeye Trail where it crosses the stream on a bridge. Turn left, away from the creek, and climb gradually out of the valley. Stay on the blue-blazed Buckeye Trail as it turns right on a narrow, level path, avoiding the broad trail ahead that continues to climb. Soon your trail, too, resumes a gradual ascent.

Pass the amphitheater on your left. Come out of the woods at the big parking lot where you began this hike.

# French Creek Reservation

## A loop through the forested French Creek valley

*Hiking distance: 3¾ miles*
*Hiking time: 2 hours*
*Maps: USGS Avon; reservation map*

Dense forests and the shaly gorges of three creeks highlight this circuit hike in French Creek Reservation, a 428-acre unit of the Lorain County Metropolitan Park District. The hiking is not too strenuous even for children, who will delight in the interpretive center where exhibits and live animals help teach the ways of nature. The facility has a large auditorium, seasonal displays, a nature gift shop, classrooms for nature study, a nonlending library, and a deck overlooking French Creek.

The center not only features interesting lectures and exhibits, but also serves as a jumping-off point for excursions into the surrounding woods and gorges. Recent program listings included events ranging from an illustrated talk on the wreck of the *Edmund Fitzgerald* to an exhibit of waterfowl art, a program on bats for elementary school children, an adult hike to examine plant reproduction, and a field trip for preschoolers to collect aquatic insects in French Creek.

## Access

French Creek Reservation is in Sheffield. The trailhead for this hike is at the French Creek Nature Center on OH 611 (Colorado Avenue). The nature center is open daily 8–4:30, with extended hours on Thursday until 9 PM.

## Trail

As you face the nature center, find the paved path on your right leading off the parking area at a sign that reads "Trail." Your way

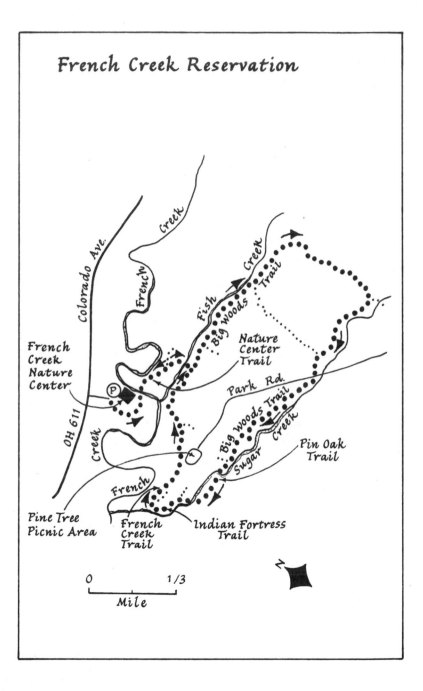

French Creek Reservation

*Sugar Creek has cut deeply into the underlying rock to form a scenic ravine.*

curves around the building and then turns right on the Nature Center Trail to descend steps into the French Creek gorge. Cross the creek on a bridge and climb to an observation platform overlooking the hemlock-studded ravine. Follow the Nature Center Trail as it turns right for a gentle drop into the Fish Creek valley. Cross the creek and climb steps to reach a T-intersection with the Big Woods Trail. You will return to this spot later; for now, turn left.

The Big Woods Trail heads east on a terrace above Fish Creek, called Walker Ditch upstream of the reservation. Pass the Salt Lick Trail on your right. Farther along, continue straight on a narrow footpath where the wide and well-graded trail goes right. The way eventually curves right, away from Fish Creek, and passes through a forest of tall pin and red oaks before reaching Sugar Creek. Do not cross the stream, but rather turn right to follow a trail paralleling the little creek on an upper terrace. Rejoin the wider portion of the Big Woods Trail and continue straight.

Cross a paved road that follows an old railroad grade through the park. Keep left at trail junctions to remain close to Sugar Creek, known as Jungbluth Ditch beyond the park's boundaries. Reach an intersection and turn left. Where the Big Woods Trail curves right, keep straight on the Pin Oak Trail. Descend to cross Sugar Creek at a picturesque stretch where the water has cut a small gorge through shale cliffs. The Pin Oak Trail narrows as it turns right where a broad trail goes straight. The way descends to again cross Sugar Creek. Climb to reach the Indian Fortress Trail and turn left.

Follow the Indian Fortress Trail as it hairpins to the right rear and then turn left on the French Creek Trail. Soon reach the paved road that encircles Pine Tree Picnic Area. Go left and walk along the road. Turn into the first parking area on your left and find a wood-chipped footpath (the Nature Center Trail) at the right rear of the lot. You reenter the forest after passing horseshoe courts on your left. Soon the Big Woods Trail joins from the right rear. The way circles around a parking lot. Turn left to keep on the Nature Center Trail, cross Fish and French Creeks, and return to the nature center.

# Spencer Lake
# Wildlife Area
## Around Spencer Lake and
## along the Black River

*Hiking distance: 2 miles*
*Hiking time: 1 hour*
*Maps: USGS Lodi; Buckeye Trail, Medina section*

Spencer Lake Wildlife Area is located at the eastern edge of the Till Plains, an immense region in North America's midsection that fans out westward from the Appalachian Plateau in Ohio to the Great Plains of South Dakota, Nebraska, and Kansas. About 2 miles east of Spencer Lake, a low escarpment marks the end of the plains and the beginning of the mountains. From here west, the Till Plains extend more than 800 miles, comprising one of the most fertile farming areas of the country.

On the glaciated plains, the grinding ice leveled the bedrock hills and filled the valleys with till or glacial drift—a blanket of unsorted earth, gravel, and sand. Deep, rich soils formed in material laid down by the ice or in material deposited in shallow lakes that existed after the glaciers melted. The resulting landscape of the Till Plains is remarkably flat, typified by terrain that is nearly level or gently sloping. The greatest topographic relief is usually found along watercourses, such as the East Branch of the Black River that curls near Spencer Lake. The winding stream has cut down through the till, dissecting the plains and carving picturesque bluffs.

Your trail circles impounded Spencer Lake in a counterclockwise direction. Sections of the path are very wet during rainy months. Hunting is allowed in the 618-acre wildlife area, so exercise caution during big-game season.

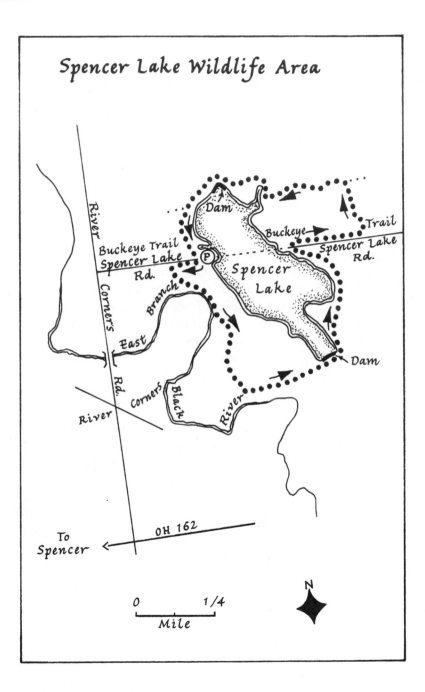

Spencer Lake Wildlife Area

## Access

Spencer Lake Wildlife Area is in Spencer Township, Medina County. From Spencer, drive east on OH 162 for 1.5 miles. Turn left on River Corners Road. Pass through the hamlet of River Corners, bridge the East Branch of the Black River, and turn right on Spencer Lake Road (1.2 miles from OH 162). The road ends in 0.3 mile at a parking area and a boat-launch ramp on the shore. A pedestrian causeway extends across Spencer Lake.

## Trail

Return along Spencer Lake Road about 1/10 mile. The Buckeye Trail follows the road, having crossed Spencer Lake on the causeway. Turn left on a wide track that leads into an upland forest. The entryway is blocked by a cable slung between two posts. The trail curves to reach the bluff above the East Branch of the Black River. Trees shading the path are mostly sugar maple, American beech, basswood, black cherry, and red oak. Tall pawpaw forms the understory in small, low areas.

Farther along, after leaving the river behind, the trail runs between an agricultural field on your right and woods on your left. At the far edge of the farm field, turn left and follow a broad, mowed swath through a thicket of multiflora rose and then along an old field of goldenrods, tall ironweed, vervain, Indian hemp, and milkweed. Reenter the forest.

The trail comes out of the woods and crosses the low, earthen dam at the south end of Spencer Lake. The lake lies at an elevation of 847 feet and the Appalachian foothills to the east rise more than 200 feet higher. Curve left off the dam to follow the east shore of the impoundment along a broad trail. The way narrows as you reach the trees; take the path farthest from the water. The trail becomes wider and more worn as you approach the eastern parking area and boat launch.

Turn right on the paved eastern extension of Spencer Lake Road. Walk about 1/4 mile along the road (which is also the Buckeye Trail), then turn left on a broad, mowed lane; an old field is on your left and a scrubby forest is on your right. Pass between two ponds, with another pond off to the right front. In this area, reach a

*Spencer Lake offers simple, quiet outdoor recreation. (Beverly J. Brown)*

T-intersection and turn left. The way goes through fields and brush-land, then enters the forest.

Descend gradually to within sight of the water, then go right, following the trail through the woods. Cross a low area and come out of the trees at the dam at the north end of the lake. Walk across the low, earthen dam and curve left. Keep straight, close to the water, where a broad side trail goes right. You will soon reach the parking lot.

# The Flats

## Walking and a boat excursion in Cleveland

*Hiking distance: 1 mile*
*Hiking time: 1 hour*
*Map: USGS Cleveland South*

The Cuyahoga River curls through a flat bottomland as it nears its end at Lake Erie. Cleveland, the Western Reserve's largest city, grew up at the river's mouth. The river and the surrounding flats have witnessed most of the historic events associated with Cleveland's two centuries.

Moses Cleaveland and his crew of surveyors landed on the right (east) bank of the river on July 22, 1796. Cleaveland proclaimed this the "Capital Town of the Western Reserve" and allowed his men to name the town after him rather than after the river. Less than a year later, on May 2, 1797, Lorenzo and Rebecca Carter, along with their five children and Rebecca's brother, Ezekial Hawley, arrived from Vermont. They built a log cabin on the Flats a short distance upriver from Cleaveland's landing site; a small band of friendly Senecas lived on the left bank. Hawley soon moved inland to the heights to escape the mosquitoes, but the Carters stayed, becoming Cleveland's first permanent white settlers. Samuel Huntington, arriving from Norwich, Connecticut, spent the night of October 7, 1800, with the Carters. He wrote in his diary, ". . . they have the fever."

The Senecas left in 1805 after other tribes surrendered their western Ohio lands in the Treaty of Fort Industry. Lorenzo Carter died in 1814. In 1827, Rebecca passed on, 30 years after settling in the Western Reserve and the year the Ohio & Erie Canal reached Cleveland. The canal emptied into the Cuyahoga at lock 44, downriver from the site of the Carter cabin.

With the coming of the canal, the Flats became the commercial and economic center of Cleveland. Ship chandlers, fish stores, and manufacturers set up business along the river and canal. Industries—

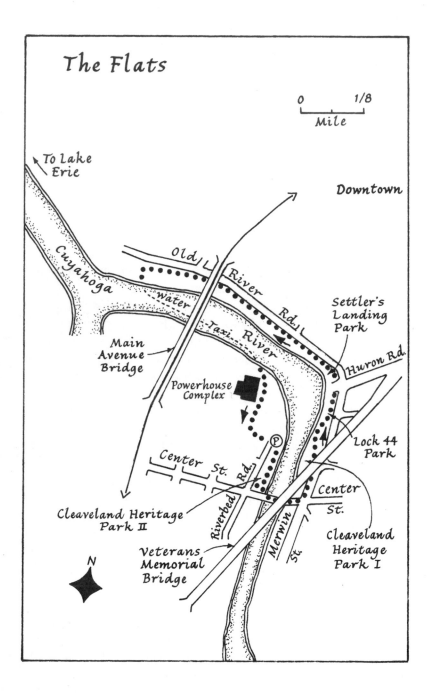

The Flats

0   1/8
Mile

To Lake Erie

Downtown

Cuyahoga

Old River Rd.

Water

Taxi River

Main Avenue Bridge

Settler's Landing Park

Huron Rd.

Powerhouse Complex

Lock 44 Park

Center St.

Riverbed Rd.

Center St.

Cleaveland Heritage Park II

Merwin St.

Cleaveland Heritage Park I

Veterans Memorial Bridge

N

flour mills, steel mills, railroads, warehousing—grew in the area. John D. Rockefeller started the Standard Oil Company in the Flats in 1870 and Sherwin-Williams opened its first paint factory on Canal Street in 1873. The Flats flourished economically for over 100 years. By the 1950s, the heavy industrial center of the Flats extended upriver beyond the city limits 5 miles south. However, in the past 35 years, the Flats have changed dramatically. Decay began to settle over the river in the 1960s as businesses closed, pared back operations, or moved to the Sun Belt. The city and valley hit bottom when the infamous Cuyahoga River fire occurred in 1969. The river burned at a railroad crossing in the Flats upstream of your walk.

The Women's City Club adopted the neglected Flats in 1972 and spearheaded efforts to establish parks on both sides of the Cuyahoga. In 1976 they built a replica of the Carter cabin as the centerpiece of Cleaveland Heritage Park I. By the late 1980s, entertainment areas had sprung up in the old factories and warehouses. Today a cleaner river attracts boating enthusiasts and the Flats once again throb with the city's economic success.

This short walk explores part of the historic Flats, now a lively shopping, dining, and recreational district. Cleveland's demeanor is an interesting mix of friendly midwestern town and busy metropolis. After dark, the glittering restaurants, nightclubs, and bars drive the city's revitalization. It is the best place in Cleveland for what the French call *flâner,* to stroll and see other people. During the day, the old industrial character of the Flats reasserts itself, especially in the area upriver of the Veterans Memorial Bridge. The valley remains a working area of manufacturers, fish stores, ship chandlers, and warehouses. By night or day, the Flats reflect the enduring toughness and ethnic diversity of a great urban center.

## Access

Parking is often hard to find in the Flats. You may be fortunate enough to park along Riverbed Road in the vicinity of Cleaveland Heritage Park II. If not, leave your car as close as possible and make your way to the park lying on the Cuyahoga's left (west) bank, which serves as the trailhead for this walk.

## Trail

Cleaveland Heritage Park II, the second riverfront park built by the Women's City Club, was dedicated in 1981. It lies in the shadow of the old Baltimore and Ohio Railroad bridge. This jackknife bridge is a type popular at the turn of the century but now obsolete. It was designed by bridge engineer William Scherzer of Chicago and is now kept permanently open to allow ships to pass. A hinged counterweight keeps the bridge in balance. Completed in 1907, it is the longest single-leaf Scherzer bridge ever built, 334 feet in total length with a clear channel width of 210 feet.

Walk upriver through the park. This park and others on your walk combine superlative views of the river and the downtown skyline a few blocks east. During the warm months, traffic on the river ranges from canoes, rowboats, and racing sculls to pleasure boats of all sizes and 600-foot lake freighters. Continue a short distance along Riverbed Road to Center Street. Turn left and cross the Cuyahoga on the Center Street bridge. The span rotates on a pier in either a clockwise or counterclockwise direction. Built in 1901, it is the last remaining swing bridge on the river.

Soaring above the Center Street bridge is the high-level Veterans Memorial Bridge. Three years under construction, the viaduct ranked as the largest double-decked concrete bridge in the world when it opened in 1918. The 3112-foot-long span originally carried four lanes of automobile traffic on the upper deck (widened to six lanes in 1967–69) and four streetcar tracks on the lower deck. The streetcars ceased operation in 1954. The first nonmovable bridge constructed in the Flats, it is listed on the National Register of Historic Places.

Once across the Center Street bridge, turn left on Merwin Street and again pass under the Veterans Memorial Bridge. On the river bank is Cleaveland Heritage Park I and the reconstructed Carter log cabin. The replica is open June through August on Wednesday, Friday, and Saturday 11–4 and on Sunday 1–5; free.

Adjacent to the Carter cabin is Lock 44 Park, commemorating the site of the northern terminus of the Ohio & Erie Canal. The old lock has been filled in, but the abutment at the river's edge is part of

*The jackknife Scherzer bridge (1907) and the Powerhouse (1892)*

the wharf where cargo was transferred between canal boats and lake freighters.

Lock 44 Park offers a good vantage point for views up- and downriver. The Cuyahoga is here near the finish of its 100-mile journey from the highlands in Geauga County. The river ends as a tame flow into Lake Erie, with its final 5 or 6 miles dredged to a depth of 25 feet for commercial lake shipping. The US Army Corps of Engineers dredges daily to maintain the navigation channel.

Continue along Merwin Street, cross Huron Road, and walk down Old River Road. On your left is Settler's Landing Park, the site where Moses Cleaveland stepped ashore in 1796. The park was developed as part of Cleveland's bicentennial celebration in 1996. Beyond the landing site, Old River Road is lined with 19th- and 20th-century commercial buildings.

Walk under the high-level Main Avenue bridge, a truss cantilever structure that was built in 1939. The bridge is 8000 feet in length and is connected by a golden rivet at its center. Nestled between the massive supports under the span is the little building of the city's Bureau of Bridges and Docks, a juxtaposition of the splendid and the simple.

Continue to near the end of Old River Road. Here you can turn and walk back to Cleaveland Heritage Park II or you can boat across the Cuyahoga aboard the Holy Moses Water Taxi, which runs regularly among four stops. This pedestrian ferry operates May through October from a dock between the Beach Club and the Longhorn Steakhouse on Thursday (6 PM–1 AM), Friday (6 PM–2 AM), Saturday (noon–2 AM), and Sunday (noon–11 PM). Take the boat to the Powerhouse/Nautica entertainment complex.

If you sail across the river, you dock in front of the immense, four-level, brick Powerhouse (1892), originally the Woodland Avenue and West Side Street Railroad Powerhouse. Built by Marcus Hanna, it served as a power source for the city's streetcar system. The two 240-foot-high smokestacks were added in 1901. The building was slated for demolition, but it was saved in 1988 and adapted for use as an entertainment palace. The Powerhouse is on the National Register of Historic Places.

Make your way around the Nautica Stage and arrive back at Cleaveland Heritage Park II.

# Geneva
# State Park
## Of marshes and marinas

*Hiking distance: 3½ miles*
*Hiking time: 2 hours*
*Map: USGS Geneva*

O f all the landscape features found in the Western Reserve, perhaps none is as important or as maligned as wetlands. They are a legacy of the last Ice Age, "a signature of time and eternity" in the words of Carl Sandburg. Wetlands are dotted across the Reserve on old glacial flats, on former lake bottoms, in valleys, and around the margins of lakes and ponds.

All wetlands serve valuable natural functions, but the marshes that embroider Lake Erie give irreplaceable benefits throughout the entire basin. They buffer shorelines from erosive effects of storms and abnormally high waves, trap sediment, recycle nutrients, and serve as nurseries for mollusks, insects, fish, amphibians, reptiles, birds, and mammals. Marshes along the shores of big lakes like Erie are by far the biologically richest and most productive of all the lake habitats.

Before wetlands were recognized as one of the most valuable ecosystems on earth, they were drained, filled, flooded, degraded, clear-cut, and plowed. Ohio's wetlands suffered disproportionately. Agriculture, commercial exploitation, and growing population demands accelerated their destruction. Depending on the authority, Ohio is either first or second in the nation in wetlands loss. Between 90 and 95 percent of the Buckeye State's wetlands have been destroyed. Only California may have wiped out more.

Today some wetlands are protected by federal and state laws, but the country as a whole continues to give up about 350,000 acres each year, primarily to developers. To stem the tide of decline, the government sometimes requires the mitigation (creation) of new

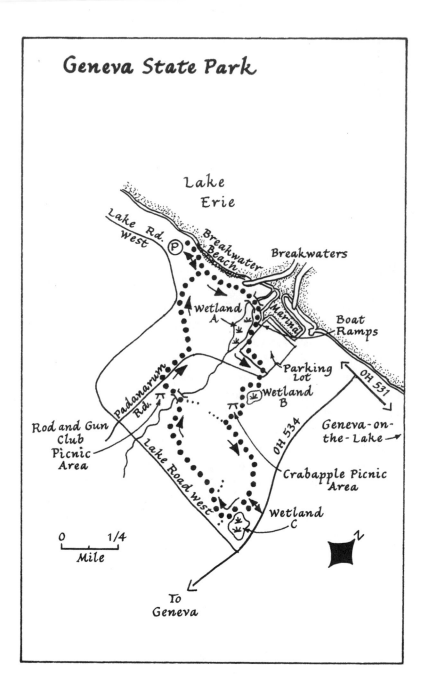

wetlands to replace those filled during development. Geneva State Park serves as a good example of the mitigation policy because created wetlands were engineered by the state to replace marshes lost during construction of a marina on the Lake Erie shore. The new wetlands are larger than those destroyed but most of them are far inland, so the lake has lost their benefit. This walk explores the former natural area and the human-created wetlands.

The marsh versus marina showdown was set as early as 1945 when Congress authorized the establishment of harbors along Lake Erie "for light draft commercial and fishing vessels and for recreational craft." Geneva-on-the-Lake was identified in a 1969 report as an ideal location for a small-boat harbor since a state park was being established in the area. Congress appropriated money for the Geneva-on-the-Lake marina in 1978.

Before the initial appropriation, the Ohio Department of Natural Resources (DNR) had built a mammoth 1800-car parking lot in the mid-1970s for the state park swimming beach. A shore marsh was filled in for the parking area and adjacent wetlands were dug out to provide dirt for the fill. This was before wetlands received protection by law.

By the early 1980s, support for the marina was mushrooming. Boaters, elected county and local officials, the Ohio DNR, and the US Army Corps of Engineers (who would build the facility) were all in favor of construction. There was no apparent opposition. The state government lobbied the Ohio congressional delegation to allocate more federal funds. In the meantime, new environmental laws protecting wetlands had come on the books. The army recognized that the marina plans as originally conceived would have an impact on wetlands in the park. The federal government implemented a "reformulation phase" of the project to examine environmental effects. The Ohio DNR fought stiffly to preserve its big parking lot by recommending that more marshland be erased for the marina. The US Fish and Wildlife Service (USFWS) stepped in and identified the Erie marshes as a "significant natural area." A survey by USFWS biologists found far more birds breeding in the lake marshes than anywhere else in the park. The USFWS urged that the remaining wetlands be saved and that the parking lot be dug up to build the new marina.

*Normally serene, Lake Erie can change in hours when storms blow up.*

The government, in its wisdom, sawed the baby in half. The marina was built by destroying half of the marsh and half of the parking lot. The USFWS won the concession that the wetlands loss would be mitigated by enhancing and expanding the damaged marsh next to the new marina. This became known as "Wetland A" in government environmental documents. Two other mitigated wetlands (called B and C) were later built in the interior of the park. Wetland B mostly flooded the park's Green Heron Nature Trail. The pathway was discontinued and not relocated or rebuilt.

The state park kept its swimming beach east of the new marina, but was forced to abandon it a few years later. Water pollution from the boat traffic proved anew that power craft and swimmers cannot coexist. A more serious problem for the beach itself was the severe erosion created by the stone jetties jutting into the lake to protect the boat entrance. The massive, long walls prevented the transport of replacement sand eastward along the shore. The Ohio DNR built a new swimming area, Breakwater Beach, west of the marina, where natural sand transport was trapped by the jetties.

Your walk leads past all of these landmarks: Breakwater Beach, Wetland A, the marina, the big parking lot, Wetland B, remnants of the Green Heron Trail, and Wetland C. It offers a lot of variety in a relatively short distance: the Lake Erie shoreline, estuarine-type lagoons, interior marshes and swamps, meadows, young woods and thickets, older forests, and the human-made developments that overlie the land.

In spring and wet seasons, parts of the trail are very muddy and water-filled. Hunting is allowed along sections of the trail, so hiking here should be avoided during big-game season. In winter, snowmobiles use some of these paths.

## Access

From US 20 in downtown Geneva, travel north on OH 534 for 3 miles. Turn left on Lake Road West into Geneva State Park. Continue straight across the intersection with Padanarum Road and follow Lake Road West past the entrance to Breakwater Beach on your right. Pull into the next parking area on your right, 1.6 miles from OH 534. This lot serves as the park's snowmobile staging area in winter.

## Trail

Walk toward the lake through a broad, grassy opening. Near the low bluff, turn right on a narrow path. Strong northwest waves cause persistent erosion in this area, and various control devices have been constructed to slow the crumbling of the shore. Breakwaters, jetties, groins, and concrete slabs anchor the gravelly strand, but big trees on the palisade still topple into the water. Their logs create a jumbled barrier on the narrow, cobbled beach. Occasional cuts in the bluff enable you to go down to the water and explore.

Your trail very shortly reaches the Breakwater Beach parking lot. Continue along the lake. On the other side of the parking area, you can either walk down a broad trail to the swimming beach or continue on a gravel lane that leads through the woods. Either way will lead you to the opposite side of the beach, where you cross the low, landward end of a stone breakwater.

Walk through sand dunes dotted with beach pea and small sumac and cottonwood saplings. A marshy lagoon lies behind the lake on your left. Leave the dunes, go through a little field, cross a narrow drainageway on a short, grated bridge, and turn right, away from the lake.

You are now walking on a levee separating the enhanced and enlarged Wetland A on your right from the marina on your left. The right-hand view probably resembles the scene from the early part of this century when a local naturalist described it as "the best beach-dune area of the county." The 383-slip marina, the six-lane boat ramp, the 812-car paved parking lot, and the stone jetties provide dramatic contrast. Tall poles with lights are visible at night from all parts of the park and beyond. Go past the boat ramp on your left and veer left toward the back of the big parking lot.

Do not take the road that leads south out of the boat-ramp area. Rather, turn left onto a drive with a sign reading "Boat Trailer Parking Only" and walk east along the south edge of the parking lot until it spills out into the easternmost exit/entrance road. Turn right, walk to the stop sign at Padanarum Road, angle left across the road, and enter the forest on a broad trail blocked by a cable strung between poles.

The woods road leads shortly to a dam backing up a pond punctuated with dead snags of flooded trees. This is the 3-acre mitigated Wetland B. Pick up a narrow path to the right of the dam and skirt the wetlands, keeping them on your left. This path is a remnant of the old Green Heron Nature Trail. The way curves to the right away from the pond, broadens, and enters Crabapple Picnic Area. Walk past a wooden-shingled shelter and immediately turn left onto a broad trail behind a drinking fountain.

Stay on the wide path until it comes out of the woods into a shrubby field and meets a cross trail. Turn left. The old field is gradually being overtaken by saplings of elms, willows, cottonwood, sour gum, and red maple. Dogwoods, sumacs, and viburnums form scattered, dense thickets, favored places for hornets to build their big paper nests. Frogs abound in the many low, wet places in the field. They in turn attract snakes, which can be seen slithering off the trail at your approach. The meadow is especially colorful in late summer and autumn when the asters, daisies, and goldenrods are in bloom and butterflies flutter from flower to flower. The park has placed bluebird nesting boxes in the field. The quiet hiker will likely encounter deer in this area.

Your trail is a broad mowed swath through the field. It serves as a snowmobile route in winter. The path curves gradually to the right. Follow the first short spur to your left that leads to a dam and a pond near OH 534. This is 6-acre Wetland C, the third mitigated area designed to replace the lakeshore marshes lost during construction of the marina. It is similar to B—open water with dead trees and tangled thickets, ringed with sedges and cattails. Return along the spur to the main trail and turn left.

Shortly beyond, turn right onto another broad mowed swath. Continue for some distance, but turn left into the woods on a narrow path at the first opportunity, leaving the field and the snowmobile trail behind. Rusty fences and apple trees remain from the days when this area was an orchard. The way leads you through a small Scots pine plantation, then descends slightly to a T-intersection. Turn left, cross a little creek on a bridge, and climb up to the Rod and Gun Club Picnic Area.

Pass through the picnic area and turn right on Padanarum Road. Walk about 1/10 mile, then turn left on a paved park service road where Padanarumx Road goes sharply right.

Follow the service road to its junction with Lake Road West. Turn right and walk about 800 feet to the entrance to Breakwater Beach. Turn right here, go through the parking lot, and pick up the shore trail on the lake bluff. A turn to the left will lead you back to the snowmobile staging area

# The Plateau

*Chapin Forest Reservation (Beverly J. Brown)*

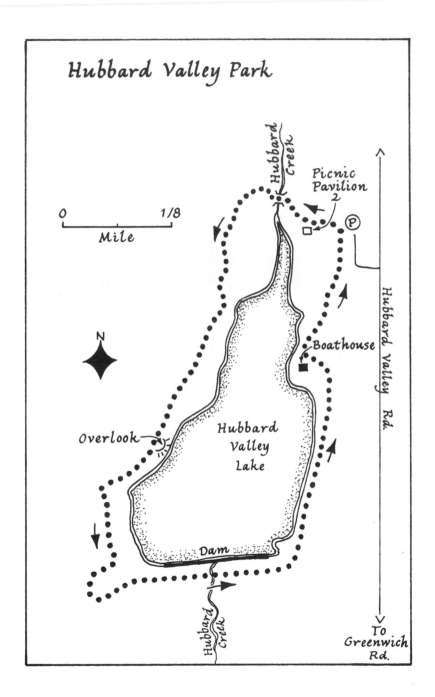

# Hubbard Valley Park

Hubbard Creek

Picnic Pavilion
2

0    1/8
Mile

P

Hubbard Valley Rd.

N

Boathouse

Overlook

Hubbard
Valley
Lake

Dam

Hubbard Creek

To
Greenwich
Rd.

# Hubbard Valley Park

## A circuit walk in the Muskingum River watershed

*Hiking distance: 1¼ miles*
*Hiking time: 45 minutes*
*Map: USGS Seville; park map*

The Muskingum Valley is the largest watershed wholly within Ohio, covering nearly one-fifth of the state. The Muskingum River basin extends as far north as Akron and as far west as Mansfield, draining an area of more than 8000 square miles. The south-flowing Muskingum is fed by many tributaries before finally discharging into the Ohio River at Marietta.

Virtually every part of the basin is controlled by the Muskingum Watershed Conservancy District, a quasi-governmental organization formed in 1933 to prevent flooding and to enhance conservation practices. In the 1930s that meant the construction of dams, a component of the massive public works program fueled by the federal government as part of an unemployment relief plan. In the Muskingum Valley, about 8000 men found work in the labor-creating project. They built 14 dams in 5 years at a cost of $50 million in federal, state, and local funds.

The Conservancy District gradually extended its control up many of the myriad smaller streams into the headwaters of the basin. In 1960 it established the Chippewa Subdistrict in the Chippewa Creek watershed in the south-central portion of the Western Reserve. The Chippewa Subdistrict covers almost 200 square miles and consists of eight dams and 32 miles of channelized streams. One of the dams is on Hubbard Creek near its source in southern Medina County. Hubbard, which flows south into Chippewa Creek, was tamed in 1980 with a "floodwater retarding structure III-A." The Medina

County Park District created Hubbard Valley Park, with the flood-control reservoir as its dominant physical feature, in 1981. Funds to maintain the Hubbard Creek dam and other water-control developments in the Chippewa Subdistrict are generated through a maintenance tax levied against the properties downstream of the dams.

## Access

Hubbard Valley Park is in Guilford Township near Seville. Head north through Seville on OH 3 and turn right on Greenwich Road. Drive east on Greenwich Road for 0.7 mile to the first intersection and turn left on Hubbard Valley Road. The park entrance is on the left after 1.0 mile. Turn right off the short entrance drive into the parking lot and park on the far end.

## Trail

Head toward Picnic Pavilion 2, keep it on your left, and find your path at a sign that reads "Nature Trail" with an arrow pointing the way. The trail makes a sharp left turn into the woods, crosses Hubbard Creek on an arched bridge, turns right, and angles away from the stream.

Your way is a broad trail through a mixed-age forest of sugar maple, American beech, shagbark hickory, tulip tree, black cherry, hornbeam, and ironwood. A short spur leads left to a bench on a knoll overlooking the reservoir.

Come out of the forest into a floodway carpeted with grasses and wildflowers. Climb out of the floodway and turn right through a grove of white ash. The path curves left through a second-growth forest and comes out into the open again as it heads toward I-76.

Turn left near the interstate right-of-way and cross the 50-foot-high earthen dam that holds back Hubbard Creek. The little stream can be seen below on your right flowing from pipes at the dam's foot. The dam is mowed annually to control woody vegetation, which could cause a structural problem to the fill on the framework. Thickets of reeds and small willows along the shore are favored nesting sites for red-winged blackbirds, reportedly Ohio's most common bird. The brilliantly marked males may fly out to challenge your

*Hubbard Valley Park was created around a flood control reservoir.*

approach if you walk here in the spring. Once across the dam, the trail turns left to continue around the reservoir.

Come to the recreational complex of the park—boathouse, dock, picnic area, and picnic shelter. The reservoir is managed for recreational fishing and is stocked with northern pike, largemouth bass, crappies, and channel catfish. Turn left to follow the shoreline, keep the boathouse on your left, and reach a paved trail along the water. Walk right, crossing a ravine on a bridge, and return to the parking lot.

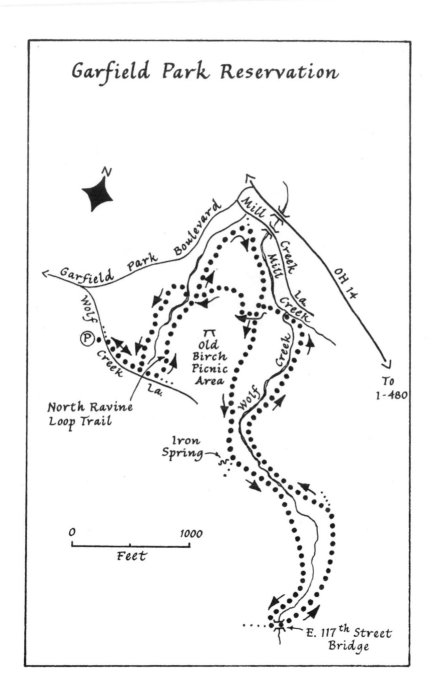

Garfield Park Reservation

# Garfield
# Park Reservation

### A circuit hike through an old park
### rich in scenery and history

*Hiking distance: 2½ miles*
*Hiking time: 1½ hours*
*Maps: USGS Shaker Heights; park map*

Garfield Park became the 12th reservation of Cleveland Metroparks in 1986, but its founding goes back to 1896 when the City of Cleveland purchased farmland at the tattered edge of the Allegheny Plateau in Newburgh Township as a place where city residents could enjoy the countryside. Walking paths, clay tennis courts, ball diamonds, a swimming pool, and two ponds were built. Visitation swelled, especially after 1915 when the Cleveland Railway Company extended its streetcar tracks from downtown to make a scenic loop through the park.

Encroaching development and urbanization tossed Garfield Park into a spiraling decline after World War II. By the 1970s, many of the original recreational features had disappeared, the boating ponds were choked with silt, and all the fish in the park's creeks had been killed by industrial pollutants and leaking sanitary sewers.

Today Garfield Park is again an attractive open space where city and suburban dwellers can enjoy the countryside. Picnic areas and playing fields are being maintained, the trail network has been expanded and blazed, a wildlife preserve has been set aside, and a new nature center opened in 1987. The century-old park belongs now to the suburbs, but it attests to an earlier landscape that once was country.

This loop walk follows three hiking trails to explore the reservation's thickly forested ridges and ravines. You will pass several historic landmarks and walk along part of the old streetcar scenic loop. Dogs must be on a leash.

## Access

From the junction of I-480 and OH 14 in Garfield Heights, drive west on OH 14 for just over 1 mile. Turn left on Garfield Park Boulevard and enter the reservation. Follow the road for 0.3 mile to the top of the hill, then turn left on Wolf Creek Lane. Drive about 0.2 mile and pull into the second entrance on the right. The parking lot is the old trolley turnaround used by streetcars until 1948.

## Trail

Cross Wolf Creek Lane and turn right on the paved all purpose trail. Walk a short distance, passing a foot trail (your return path) and the head of a wooded ravine on your left, then turn left on a trail entering the woods just before you reach the open fields of Old Birch Picnic Area. This is the North Ravine Loop Trail.

The ravine deepens on your left as the path keeps to the ridge top. Walk through a mature forest of beech, sugar maple, red oak, black cherry, and tulip tree. Scattered white pine and hemlock can also be found. Your path intersects a cross trail. The North Ravine Loop Trail descends left into the little valley and the path from the right is your return, but for now keep straight on a connecting trail.

Soon the way descends rather steeply and comes out of the woods at the bottom of the hill onto a broad paved lane. Turn right. The pavement follows the route of the streetcar loop, which operated through the park from 1915 to 1936. Streetcars continued to serve Garfield Park from the city for 12 more years, but they no longer made the scenic loop.

Mill Creek runs along your trail on the left, but it is soon left behind. The first building that you see across the stream is the Garfield Park Nature Center.

Intersect the Iron Spring Loop Trail where it comes up steps from the left to join the old road. You will return to this spot later, but for now keep straight on the pavement. Very shortly you will pass stone stairs on your right that lead up to Old Birch. Farther along, pass another trail in an open area on your right that leads to the parking area at Old Birch. The forest grows more dense, but meadows and old fields are maintained in places by the Park District to

*Wolf Creek in Garfield Park Reservation*

provide varying habitat for wildlife. You meet Wolf Creek on your left as it tumbles down its little gorge on the way to Mill Creek.

Old Iron Spring arises on your right in a small glen amid a jumble of moss-covered boulders. Mineral water from the spring was once believed to have medicinal qualities. In the late 1800s and early 1900s, visitors collected the water and carried it home to Cleveland. Depletion of groundwater by urban development has changed the spring's gushing water to a slow seep. A side trail leads up steps past the spring, but your way continues straight on the paved lane along the creek.

The remains of an old sandstone quarry are noticeable to the observant hiker. The shallow pits and low mounds on the right of the trail are now clothed with big trees. Some of the stones used to construct the stairs and walls in the park were quarried here.

Your trail enters an especially beautiful section of the Wolf Creek ravine. The little stream has cut through layers of sandstone and created small overhanging ledges above the water. In winter, blue icicles hang suspended from the rocks. In summer, deep green mosses accentuate the coolness that lingers here even on hot days. The soft sounds of water cascading down flumes and over small riffles add to the tranquillity. Green Springs Pool, the hallmark of Wolf Creek, is a wide, deep basin below a cap of hard sandstone. It is a place favored by mallards, and a mating pair can often be found here in springtime.

Iron Spring Trail levels as it approaches the old East 117th Street bridge. The graceful span was built in the late 1890s of sandstone quarried in Bedford, about 5 miles to the southeast. Turn left and cross the broad bridge on the paved all purpose trail. Below, Wolf Creek has channelized itself into a narrow bed of stratified sandstone.

Continue along the all purpose trail (formerly East 117th Street) to the first footpath on your left. Turn left, leaving the all purpose trail and descending gradually through outcrops of layered sandstone to near the level of Wolf Creek.

Walk downstream, passing a cross trail that leads up steps to the right to Red Oak Picnic Area and down a short series of steps to your left to an old dam site. The former dam impounded an upper pond along the creek. Your way comes out upon a low stone platform that served as a boat-launching area for a lower pond that was probably dredged around 1906. In 1907, rowboats could be rented for 25 cents an hour. Today the old pond is mostly a wet meadow, home to many wetland-loving animals such as muskrat, mallard, turtles, frogs, and aquatic insects.

Curve left across the terrace. The low stone wall on your right borders Mill Creek. A break in the wall leads across a bridge to the reservation's service center. Continue straight and cross Wolf Creek on an arched sandstone bridge. The confluence of Wolf and Mill Creeks can be seen on your right.

Cross a sluiceway and climb stone steps to arrive back on the black-topped lane. Jog left here and in a short distance turn right to climb more steps to Old Birch. At the top, turn right on a path (the short Meadow Loop Trail) and walk through a sunny meadow. Your path arcs around to the left and reaches the forest. Turn right on a narrow trail as it enters the woods and descends to the North Ravine Loop Trail. Continue straight, going down to the bottom of the ravine and wood bridge over a little creek.

Climb steeply out of the valley and reach the ridgetop. Keep the open ravine on your left in this area by always choosing the left path when faced with a side trail. The rich forest humus provides ample nutrients for spring wildflowers. Early to mid-April is the best time to find them, as they bloom quickly when the days grow warm, but before the forest canopy darkens the ground. The trail soon comes out onto the paved all purpose trail. Go right to return to your waiting car.

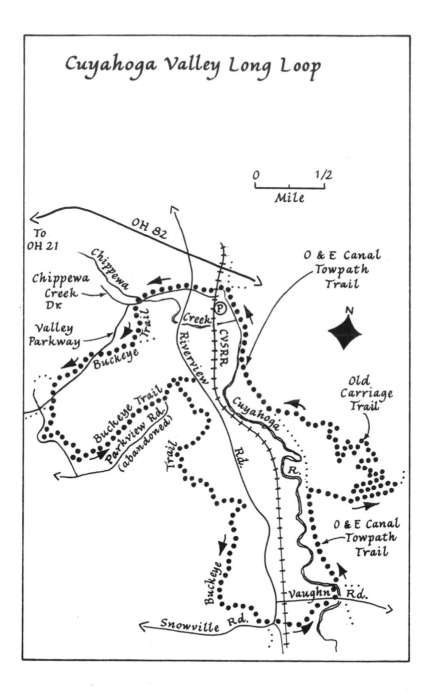

Cuyahoga Valley Long Loop

0     1/2
Mile

To OH 21

OH 82

Chippewa

Chippewa Creek Dr.

Valley Parkway

Buckeye Trail

Creek

Riverview

P

CVSRR

O & E Canal Towpath Trail

N

Buckeye Trail Parkview Rd. (abandoned)

Trail

Cuyahoga

Old Carriage Trail

R.

O & E Canal Towpath Trail

Buckeye

Vaughn Rd.

Snowville Rd.

# Cuyahoga Valley Long Loop

## A picturesque valley rich in natural and human history

*Hiking distance: 12¾ miles*
*Hiking time: 7 hours*
*Maps: USGS Northfield; Cuyahoga Valley National*
*Recreation Area; Buckeye Trail, Tinkers Creek section*

This hike features three major trails—Buckeye Trail, Ohio & Erie Canal Towpath Trail, and Old Carriage Trail—and some minor connecting trails to explore the beautiful Cuyahoga River Valley, a landscape of rumpled, forested ridges, steep-sided ravines, and flat river bottoms. The trails are in Cuyahoga Valley National Recreation Area and Brecksville Reservation.

According to The Nature Conservancy, 99 percent of the original landscape in Ohio has been altered. The Sierra Club reports that Ohio has less public land per person than any other state in the nation. Fortunately, these cheerless statistics are ameliorated somewhat in the Western Reserve. The seven counties in the heart of the Reserve (Cuyahoga, Geauga, Lake, Lorain, Medina, Portage, and Summit) rank first in the United States in the amount of parkland available to the public. A 1994 Citizens League Research Institute study showed that nearly 9 percent of the region is composed of federal, state, and locally owned parkland. These gemlike preserves are pockets of wildness encompassing more than 94,000 acres of the kind of land that has been cut, drained, filled, and developed elsewhere in the state.

The linchpin of these public holdings is the 33,000-acre Cuyahoga Valley National Recreation Area, Ohio's largest national park. When the park was created in 1974, it preserved the pastoral countryside connecting Bedford and Brecksville Reservations (in

Cleveland Metroparks) with Deep Lock Quarry, Furnace Run, Hampton Hills, and O'Neil Woods Metro Parks (units of Metro Parks, Serving Summit County). Both local park districts are establishing new parks at the north and south ends of the recreation area, thereby protecting more of the valley from continuing urbanization and spreading development.

The momentum for new parkland is largely the result of the popularity of the Ohio & Erie Canal Towpath Trail, a major long-distance trail that runs over 19 miles through the length of the recreation area. Just as the Ohio & Erie Canal provided remarkable economic growth to the region in the second quarter of the 19th century, so the reconstructed towpath is serving as a catalyst for outdoor recreational opportunities at the end of the 20th century. The towpath reopened in 1993 with a construction cost of $8 million. In 1994, over 1.4 million people—walkers, joggers, bicyclists, and equestrians—used the trail.

Your walk follows 2 miles of the Ohio & Erie Canal Towpath Trail and explores about 7 miles of the valley's other long-distance footpath, the 1200-mile trans-state Buckeye Trail. The idea for a long trail traversing Ohio was recommended by Merrill C. Gilfillan, a wildlife biologist for the Ohio Department of Natural Resources, in an article published November 2, 1958, in the *Columbus Dispatch*. Gilfillan, writing under the name Perry Cole, identified a suggested route and stated the trail "should be as endless and as boundless as the energy and the imagination of those who would use it."

Gilfillan's dream quickly became reality. The Buckeye Trail Association was formed in March 1959 and the first section of the Buckeye Trail—20 miles in southern Ohio's Hocking Hills—was dedicated in September of that year. Twenty-two years later, in 1981, the section in Brecksville Reservation—the path you will walk in this hike—was opened, thus completing a continuous footpath around the state. The Buckeye Trail is the longest circuit trail in the United States.

The third trail making up your Cuyahoga Valley long loop rewards the hiker with stately woodlands and scenic vistas of the valley. The 3¼-mile Old Carriage Trail follows part of a 20-mile network of graded carriage roads built between 1910 and 1940 by Wentworth Marshall, a Cleveland drugstore magnate.

Marshall and his wife, Louise, purchased 1000 acres of farmland in Sagamore Hills Township in the early 1900s and built a summer home called Rocky Run. Most of the old Marshall property is now a housing development, but about 400 wooded acres of the estate became part of the national recreation area.

The combination of these three trails offers excellent opportunities for observing the rich flora and the diverse wildlife of the valley, for enjoying the spectacular scenery of forest, river, and ridge, and for exploring the long history of human life in the valley.

## Access

From the center of Brecksville at the junction of OH 21 and OH 82, go east for 1.9 miles on OH 82 (past the entrance to Brecksville Reservation on your right) to the first traffic signal. Turn right on Riverview Road and descend 0.3 mile to Chippewa Creek Drive. Turn left and drive 0.1 mile to the Station Road Bridge Trailhead parking lot in the national recreation area.

## Trail

Return by foot along the entrance road, following the paved Buckeye Trail along the right shoulder. Cross the Cuyahoga Valley Scenic Railroad tracks and Riverview Road and enter Brecksville Reservation. The Buckeye Trail has been rerouted in this area since the last edition of the published guide (1988); follow the blue blazes and this updated description.

Stay on the paved all purpose trail, which soon becomes part of the physical fitness trail with rustic exercise stations set up along the way. Cross Chippewa Creek on a footbridge.

The fitness trail extends for 1½ miles, but the Buckeye Trail turns left off the paved path after station 6. Cross Chippewa Creek Drive and climb the steps into the woods just to the left of the entrance into Plateau Picnic Area.

The Buckeye Trail leads hikers on a long forest meander through a variety of habitats. At various places for short distances the trail runs

*A small waterfall plunges into a wooded ravine along the Buckeye Trail.*

along with other paths in the reservation—paved all purpose trails, broad bridle paths, and narrow hiking trails—but mostly it follows its own way through the woods. Occasionally the trail crosses or parallels park roads and pipeline rights-of-way. The Buckeye Trail is well marked with distinctive blue paint blazes on trees and other objects within 10 feet of the path. At intersections where the trail changes directions, there are two blazes, one above the other, warning of the change.

After about 1¾ miles, come upon a major junction where the Buckeye Trail splits into eastern and western segments on its way to Cincinnati. Take the left (eastern) fork, the longer, 552-mile trek to Cincinnati.

In approximately another 1¼ miles, reach an unpaved road and turn left to Ottawa Point Picnic Area. Angle right across the parking lot and reenter the woods on a single-file footpath. After falling and rising through several deep ravines, the trail comes upon abandoned Parkview Road. Follow the old road, now being reclaimed by the forest. Watch carefully for a turn to your right on a narrow path that leads through a luxuriant lowland of elms, ash, basswood, tulip tree, skunk cabbage, and ferns.

More verdant ridges and lush ravines lie ahead before the trail passes through an old field of tall grasses and wildflowers, skirting a hedgerow of ragged black willows that marks a watercourse. When you reach Snowville Road, go left. The Buckeye Trail soon turns right to continue southward to Akron and Cincinnati, but stay on the road and follow the signs to Red Lock Trailhead.

The yellow wooden buildings visible across the fields to your left mark the former hamlet of Jaite. The company houses and general store were built in 1906 for workers at the nearby Jaite Paper Mill. The factory produced bags for flour and cement. When the mill closed in the mid-1950s, the houses fell into disrepair. The National Park Service took over about 20 years later and restored the old structures. They now serve as the headquarters of Cuyahoga Valley National Recreation Area.

Your trail flanks Jaite and crosses Riverview Road. Continue straight on a graveled track through an open field. Cross the Cuyahoga Valley Scenic Railroad and pass under the electric transmission lines.

The Cuyahoga River curves into view on your right. Walk along the river, leaving the meadow and passing through a copse of American elm and box-elder. Reach Vaughn Road and turn right to cross the Cuyahoga.

On the far side, turn left (north) on the Ohio & Erie Canal Towpath Trail. Immediately on your right is Red Lock (lock 34) and beyond the lock is a short paved side trail that leads right to a small parking lot and rest rooms.

Walk north on the towpath and pass mile marker 19. It indicates the location of a historic milepost as measured from the original northern terminus of the canal near the mouth of the Cuyahoga River in Cleveland. The first shovelful of dirt was turned for construction of the Ohio & Erie Canal on July 4, 1825, near Newark in central Ohio. But it was this 38-mile section of canal between Akron and Cleveland that first opened to boat traffic just two years later, on July 4, 1827. With great ceremony, state and canal officials sailed north from Akron aboard the *State of Ohio*. Gone are the shouts and songs of the Irish immigrants who cleared the line and the snorting and clanking of mules that hauled freighters and packets up and down the canal. The "Big Ditch" shut down in 1913 after a disastrous flood in the Cuyahoga Valley swept away the canal banks and ruptured the locks. The old canal is now mucky and overgrown with large red and silver maples.

After about ¾ mile on the towpath, turn right on the Old Carriage Trail and climb out of the valley. The ¼-mile ascent gains 150 feet in elevation, gradually at first and then more steeply, on a wide trail through a dense beech-maple forest. After about another ¼ mile of level walking on the ridgetop, a bike-and-hike trail goes straight where the Old Carriage Trail turns left and narrows to a single-file footpath. Always keep left on the Old Carriage Trail when faced with a choice of paths.

The trail is mostly level for the next 1½ miles or so. Three long bridges carry you high over 80-foot-deep ravines. The steep gorges are noted for their green stands of eastern hemlock, with a few interspersed basswood, white ash, hickory, and tulip tree. The bridges provide fascinating views into the middle and upper canopies of the deep forest. They are ideal platforms for observing migrating song-birds in spring as the northbound migrants flit about the twigs and branches in search of newly emerged insects.

Begin a steep, 170-foot descent into the valley. Cross the swampy canal bed on a bridge at the toe of the slope and turn right on the towpath. Pass mile marker 18 and Whiskey Lock (lock 35). The canal locks are numbered sequentially from south to north beginning at the Portage Summit in Akron. Thus, lock 35 is the 35th lock north of Akron. Beyond the lock, the Cuyahoga comes close to your trail on the left. The mouth of Chippewa Creek can be seen across the water.

Arrive at a major trail junction and leave the towpath by turning left on the Buckeye Trail, following the signs to the Station Road Bridge Trailhead. Cross the Cuyahoga on the old Station Road bridge, now closed to vehicular traffic. Classed as a wrought-iron truss bridge, the span was built in 1881 and is an outstanding example of an early metal bridge. Iron was used for only a relatively brief period for bridge construction and was replaced by more durable steel by the end of the 19th century. The Station Road bridge is the oldest remaining metal truss bridge in the Cuyahoga Valley. Back on the left bank of the river, a short paved trail leads to the parking lot.

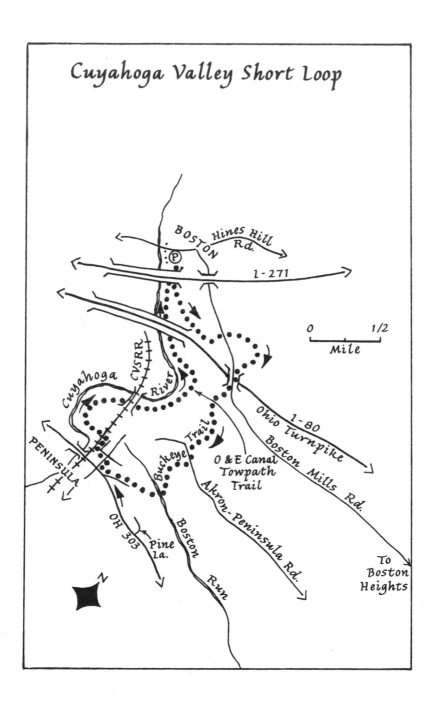

# Cuyahoga Valley Short Loop

BOSTON

Hines Hill Rd.

I-271

Cuyahoga

CVSRR

River

0    1/2
Mile

I-80

Ohio Turnpike

Boston Mills Rd.

Buckeye Trail

O & E Canal
Towpath
Trail

PENINSULA

Akron-Peninsula Rd.

OH 303

Pine La.

Boston Run

N

To
Boston
Heights

# Cuyahoga Valley
# Short Loop
### Between two old canal towns

*Hiking distance: 7¼ miles*
*Hiking time: 3½ hours*
*Maps: USGS Northfield and Peninsula; Cuyahoga Valley*
*National Recreation Area; Buckeye Trail, Akron section*

This hike features a circuit through Cuyahoga Valley National Recreation Area between Boston and Peninsula. About 4½ miles of your walk are on the blue-blazed Buckeye Trail and approximately 2½ miles follow the Ohio & Erie Canal Towpath Trail. A short connector explores some of the side streets in Peninsula.

White settlers began to push upriver through the Cuyahoga Valley from Cleveland in the early years of the 19th century. Native Americans surrendered their claim to land on the west side of the Cuyahoga River in 1805 in the Treaty of Fort Industry, thus opening the valley to the pioneers. Both Boston and Peninsula were first settled in 1806, but for years they remained only small clearings in the vast wilderness. Their destinies changed in 1827 when the Ohio & Erie Canal opened. Their location astride the inland waterway between the Great Lakes and the Gulf of Mexico brought boundless opportunities for commerce and industry.

Little Boston in the Western Reserve grew into a town with a brewery, brickyard, broom factory, gristmill, sawmill, and several stores. All of this development occurred within a span of 20 years, between 1830 and 1850.

Peninsula, about 3 miles south, experienced even greater growth. In addition to the usual assortment of industries and mills, it was also an early cheese- and butter-making center. Peninsula is the halfway point on the canal between Akron and Cleveland and also the place

*The Cuyahoga River (Beverly J. Brown)*

where the canal crosses the Cuyahoga River. Boat traffic tended to back up, creating a center for inns and hostelries catering to canal boat crews and travelers. Nearby were outcrops of select sandstone. Quarrying operations mined the rock and shipped Peninsula sandstone worldwide, starting by boat on the Ohio & Erie Canal.

Both Boston and Peninsula were home to canal boatmen and boatbuilders. Several boatbuilding yards operated in Boston. Peninsula boasted five boatyards and two dry docks. In 1863, a peak year for canal operations in the valley, 32 new canal boats were launched from Peninsula alone.

The boisterous "canawlers" put their marks on both towns as centers for lawlessness and crime. Peninsula, with five hotels and 14 taverns, was an infamous nest of drinking, gambling, and prostitution. Boston was noted for making money. The hotel in town was owned by Jim Brown, who ran a counterfeiting ring with impunity for over 30 years.

Boston and Peninsula entered an era of economic degeneration after the Civil War. The canal continued to operate, but poor management led to decreasing revenues. The coming of the railroad through the valley in 1880 was the death knell for the canal, but it brought a brief period of new prosperity for the little towns. The 20th century saw renewed decline as residents moved away to growing cities. The canal closed for good in 1913 after a disastrous flood.

Today Boston is a quiet hamlet with a white church at a fork in the road, a few private houses with low outbuildings tucked away in clusters of maple trees, and boarded-up storefronts. Midwestern novelist Theodore Dreiser's description rings true: "a part of the country . . . not as prosperous as it had once been . . . old and mildewy and reminiscent of an earlier day." The National Park Service plans to restore some of the abandoned buildings to serve as museums or exhibits. Boston is less changed by the forces of modernization than Peninsula, which has found new life as a recreational center for tourists. The village's population of about 600 is swelled on weekends by thousands of visitors who come to hike, bike, shop, eat, drink, ride the train, or ski in season. With its short side streets, old canal, and narrow 19th-century buildings, Peninsula is a village best discovered by foot. In some ways, the community fills the same role it did in the 1800s. Peninsula is comparatively tame today, but still lively and interesting, full of life and culture, history and tradition.

## Access

Drive west on Boston Mills Road from OH 8 in Boston Heights. Enter Cuyahoga Valley National Recreation Area after 1 mile and reach Boston in another 2.2 miles. Boston Trailhead is on the left after Hines Hill Road comes in from the right.

# Trail

Walk south from the trailhead, following the sign to Pine Lane. Very shortly you reach the Buckeye Trail and the Ohio & Erie Canal Towpath Trail near the high bridges that carry I-271 across the Cuyahoga Valley. Beyond the twin spans, veer left on the Buckeye Trail and climb gradually out of the valley through an old field.

The path leads you into the forest and then along I-80, the Ohio Turnpike. Come upon Boston Mills Road, turn right, walk a short distance, then turn left to reenter the woods. The path soon loops back to Boston Mills Road; turn left and cross the bridge over the turnpike. Immediately on the other side of the bridge, climb right off the road and enter a pine forest.

After 3 miles, reach Akron-Peninsula Road and turn left, walking slightly uphill. Shortly, turn right off the road into a grove of pine and spruce. The trail soon follows a hogback down into the Boston Run ravine. Follow the little creek upstream through a wide bottom punctuated with large eastern hemlock among American beech, sugar maple, and tulip tree. The path takes you across the run and ascends the north slope of the ravine.

Reach Pine Lane Trailhead. The Buckeye Trail passes through the parking lot and follows a short entrance drive under electric transmission lines. Turn right on Pine Lane, walk about 1/10 mile to the end of the road, and continue straight into the forest. The way descends into the valley, paralleling OH 303, which is visible through the trees on the left.

The trail comes out onto Dell Drive in Peninsula and continues onto Main Street (OH 303). Peninsula is listed as a historic district on the National Register of Historic Places. The Buckeye Trail continues straight on Main Street toward the river, but at the traffic signal, turn right on North Locust Street. The United Methodist Church on the corner was built in 1869. Methodists organized in Peninsula as early as 1830 but had no regular place to worship until this white-frame sanctuary was built. Across Main Street, on the southeast corner, stands the 1857 town hall, built of native sandstone quarried in the valley and considered an outstanding example of 19th-century stone architecture.

Go north one block on North Locust Street and turn left on West Mill Street, following the signs to Lock 29 Trailhead. The street curves right at the railroad station (circa 1880) of the Cuyahoga Valley Scenic Railroad. Turn left across the tracks to the Lock 29 Trailhead parking lot. On your left, the Cuyahoga River spills over the remains of an old dam built in 1832 to provide water to power a gristmill on the left bank.

Walk through the parking lot and turn right (north) on the towpath at lock 29. The structure is one of the best preserved lift locks in the valley. The original sandstone blocks have not been covered over or reinforced by concrete.

Strolling along the towpath, you have the tranquil, swampy canal on one side and, in most places screened by trees, the swift Cuyahoga River on the other. All this makes for interesting wildlife-watching. In the canal, during the warm months, turtles bask on logs and dragonflies hunt small insects. Out on the river, ducks and geese feed, while great blue herons stalk the shallows. Many birds, from colorful warblers to bald eagles, migrate along the river valley. The big, showy pileated woodpecker is a year-round resident. Almost anywhere on the canal you have a chance to see deer and beaver (or their lodges and cuttings). You soon share the passion of Pearl R. Nye, a turn-of-the-century canal boatman and balladeer who left a bountiful legacy of Ohio canal songs. Many of his songs extol the beauty of the natural world along the canal, such as the chorus from "That Old Towpath:"

> That beautiful towpath,
> Such splendor, so glorious,
> With dear Mother Nature
> I'd ramble along.

Pass lock 30, which also was the location of a feeder channel engineered to divert water from the nearby Cuyahoga River into the canal. After passing mile marker 23, the towpath tunnels under the railroad and reaches Lonesome Lock (lock 31). All the locks along the old canal were numbered and some, like Lonesome Lock, were also named. The lock is thought to have acquired its designation because of its isolated location. After the lock, the towpath is carried on a boardwalk above the marshy ground of Stumpy Basin. The basin was a wide section of the canal that allowed boats to stop over, turn around, or be put into storage for the winter when the canal was drained. The old shallow basin is now a magnificent wetland, known for its many species of rare and unusual plants.

Mile marker 22 is under the tall spans of the Ohio Turnpike. Next pass under the colossal bridges of I-271. Kids like to walk under the interstates and look up while four lanes of traffic roar high overhead. The Buckeye Trail joins the towpath at the I-271 span and your circuit is complete. Turn right on the lane to reach the Boston Trailhead.

# Sand Run
# Metro Park
## Ravines and ridges

*Hiking distance: 5½ miles*
*Hiking time: 3 hours*
*Maps: USGS Peninsula; park map;*
*Buckeye Trail, Akron section*

The summer of 1812 saw great alarm and unrest in the Western Reserve. War had broken out with Great Britain in June. Hopes for a quick victory against British forces in Canada were dashed when American General William Hull, marching from western Ohio against Fort Malden in Ontario, was outsmarted and outmaneuvered by British General Sir Isaac Brock. In August, Hull surrendered his entire command of 1900 men at Detroit without firing a shot. Ohio was left vulnerable and virtually defenseless against a strong British army in control of Detroit, a superior British naval force on Lake Erie, and vengeful Indians equipped by the British and led by the great Shawnee war chief Tecumseh.

On August 23, just one week after Hull's surrender, Major General Elijah Wadsworth, commander of the Northern Ohio Militia, assembled members of the 4th Brigade on the Green in Canfield. They had no uniforms but each man was "armed to the teeth with rifle, tomahawk and a large knife." Escorted by Captain Doud's company of Canfield Dragoons, Wadsworth set out for Cleveland in defense of the Western Reserve.

The militia marched overland to the portage trail between the Cuyahoga and Tuscarawas Rivers in present-day Akron. When they reached the portage, the brigade entered what had been Wyandot and Delaware territory as recently as seven years before. The troops camped near where Sand Run tumbles off the plateau to join the Cuyahoga River. Wadsworth posted sentries on the high ridges

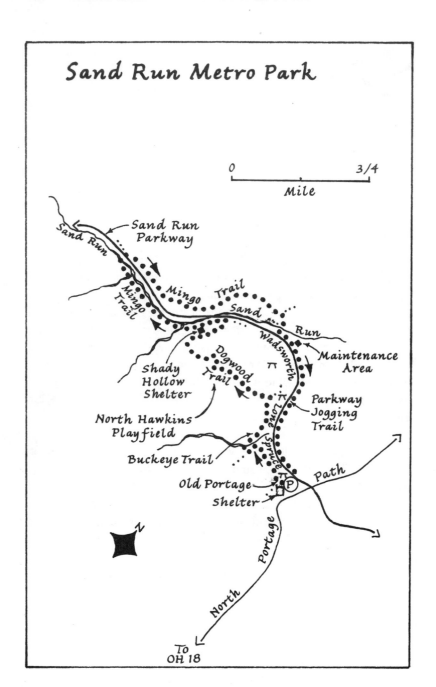

Sand Run Metro Park

overlooking the valley. The area was densely wooded, with fearsome animals such as bears and wolves still relatively common. Only a few white settlers had established scattered clearings in the great forest. To Wadsworth and his men, huddled around their fires on the flats at nightfall, the likelihood of the return of Native warriors to reclaim their lands must have seemed very real.

Wadsworth moved on from Sand Run, leading his men down the Cuyahoga to Lake Erie, where they prepared to defend the shore against any attempt at invasion. In September, some of his soldiers skirmished with a band of Indians near Point Marblehead, the first land battle of the War of 1812 in Ohio.

This circuit hike through Sand Run Metro Park begins at the site of the brigade's encampment, climbs the high ridges where the lookouts were posted, and then descends to cross Sand Run. The park is the oldest and largest of the 12 Metro Parks, Serving Summit County. It also receives by far the most visitors of any of the Metro Parks—over 1.2 million people came in 1994 alone, more than half of all the visitors to the Summit County system that year.

## Access

From downtown Akron, drive west on OH 18 (West Market Street) for 1.6 miles. Turn right on North Portage Path, the city street that follows the old Indian trail across the Continental Divide. Continue 2.3 miles, enter Sand Run Metro Park, and turn left on Sand Run Parkway. Go only about 0.1 mile and park on the left at Old Portage, the first picnic area. The 4th Brigade camped near Old Portage in 1812.

## Trail

Walk across the grassy picnic area, pass a shelter, and enter the woods on the Buckeye Trail. Your trail turns right at latrines to remain level while another path goes straight to climb uphill. Pass Lone Spruce Picnic Area on your right. The path veers left and climbs to reach more latrines at a trail junction. Turn left, then right where another trail continues straight uphill; Buckeye Trail signs help you find the way.

Your path crosses a small run on stones just upstream of a little dam. There follows a series of short, steep climbs and descents, some

*An Ohio buckeye opens its new leaves to the warm spring sun.*

with steps. The trail comes close to Sand Run Parkway and then reaches Wadsworth Picnic Area.

Keep the picnic area on your right and come to a major trail junction. The Buckeye Trail continues straight, but turn left on the Dogwood Trail as it goes uphill on steps. The Dogwood Trail reaches the ridgetop through a series of switchbacks and steps up a long, steep climb. The path comes out of the woods at the North Hawkins Playfield.

Walk along the edge of the opening, keeping the field on your left and the woods on your right. Signs help point the way. The Dogwood Trail turns right, reenters the forest, and begins a long, gradual descent on a broad path into Shady Hollow.

Pass Shady Hollow Shelter on your left. Beyond the shelter, the path is paved as it approaches a small parking lot. Cross the lot and continue along the paved entrance road, descending slightly. When Sand Run Parkway comes into view, turn left on the Mingo Trail. (The Dogwood Trail goes right at this junction.)

The Mingo Trail winds along to cross a run on a wood bridge beneath Shady Hollow Shelter. Cross two more rivulets before the trail turns sharply right and descends steeply to cross Sand Run on stones. Climb out of the streambed to a small parking area, cross Sand Run Parkway and the Parkway Jogging Trail, and begin a gradual climb. The way drops in and out of several hollows before reaching the ridgetop.

The Mingo Trail wanders through a beautiful, remote section of the park. The path is canopied with mature black cherry, tulip tree, American beech, and red oak. The way eventually comes out upon a paved road and the Buckeye Trail. Turn right and descend.

The Parkway Jogging Trail joins from the right and the road crosses Sand Run on a bridge. On the opposite side, the Buckeye and Mingo Trails turn right, but you should continue straight on the road and then left on the Parkway Jogging Trail just before the road reaches Sand Run Parkway.

The wide trail is a favorite path of walkers and runners during all months. Pass the park's maintenance area on your left. The trail parallels Sand Run Parkway except where it winds around a sandstone outcrop. The low shrubs around the rock are hobblebush, alive with bees and other pollinating insects when the flowers are blooming in July. Walk to the end of the trail at Old Portage Picnic Area.

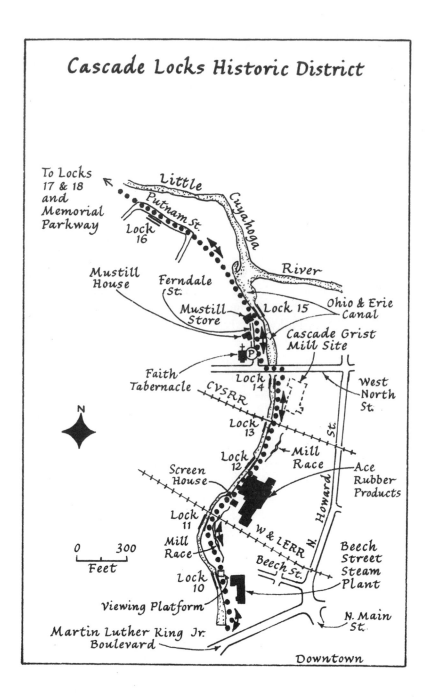

# Cascade Locks Historic District

To Locks 17 & 18 and Memorial Parkway

Little Cuyahoga River

Putnam St.

Lock 16

Mustill House

Ferndale St.

Mustill Store

Lock 15

Ohio & Erie Canal

Cascade Grist Mill Site

Faith Tabernacle

Lock 14

West North St.

CVSRR

Lock 13

Lock 12

Mill Race

N. Howard St.

Ace Rubber Products

Screen House

Lock 11

W & LERR

Mill Race

Beech Street Steam Plant

Lock 10

Beech St.

Viewing Platform

N. Main St.

Martin Luther King Jr. Boulevard

Downtown

N

0    300
Feet

# Cascade Locks Historic District

## The birthplace of Akron

*Hiking distance: 1 mile or more*
*Hiking time: 1-plus hours*
*Map: USGS Akron West*

The construction of the Ohio & Erie Canal was the most important internal improvement in Ohio's early history, contributing more to growth, progress, and unity than any other public project in the 19th century. The first section was completed in 1827 between Cleveland and Akron. The waterway provided Ohio farmers and manufacturers with their first reliable, low-cost transportation of goods to eastern and southern markets. The north-south canal cut through the heart of the Western Reserve, bringing roaring prosperity. Cleveland, at the northern terminus of the canal on Lake Erie at the mouth of the Cuyahoga River, experienced rapid, chaotic growth. Akron, at the summit of the divide, had neither lake nor navigable river, yet its boom was no less dramatic. In many ways, Akron epitomizes the quintessential canal success story. Akron was only a land speculator's dream in 1825, when canal construction began. By 1827, it was home to 600 people; by 1840, more than 2300.

The canal, starting at an elevation of 575 feet above sea level at Lake Erie, had to climb 395 feet into the Appalachian foothills in the first 30 miles. It made 200 feet of that climb in the 2-mile stretch through Akron, using as many locks getting across the town as it did coming up from Cleveland. By far the steepest section was the ascent out of the Little Cuyahoga River valley. A series of seven stair-step locks was built to lift and lower canal boats over the Continental Divide. The close-knit Cascade Locks slowed the passage of boats—it took a canal boat at least 6 hours to pass through Akron—and the falling water provided a convenient source of cheap energy for grinding grain and producing goods.

The canal plunges nearly 70 feet down the escarpment from the summit to river level in less than a third of a mile. The area became a bustling center of inns, taverns, stores, hotels, mills, and factories. Lining the canal banks at each level were dozens of canal warehouses. Prince Alexander Phillip Maximilian, passing through the city by canal boat in 1834, wrote in his diary: ". . . Akron, a considerable town in a remarkable situation. It . . . had already an extensive trade, many neat wooden houses, stores, manufacturers, an iron foundry, and an establishment where, by means of a wheel, bedsteads and other articles of furniture are turned."

Historians generally recognize that it was the locks rather than the canal itself that made Akron. But what really assured Akron's continual industrial success after canal traffic declined and then stopped was the millrace that paralleled the Cascade Locks. Water from the race powered the factories and mills up and down the valley. Akron made the transition from a water-based 19th-century industrial center to a major 20th-century production capital. The city escaped the early fate of most other towns along the canal that flourished for a short period but are now quiet villages. Akron's decline came relatively recently, when economic hard times chipped away at the city's advantage. Akron slipped down into the Rust Belt and reflected the ills that beset the nation's recession-weary towns: troubled streets, deserted factories, homes ravaged by layoffs and crime.

Yankee ingenuity and a strong work ethic long kept Akron busy and prosperous. The canal and all it meant are still there, crouching in the city's underbrush. Today the city, fueled by a strong private initiative, is attempting to redevelop the Ohio & Erie Canal as a centerpiece for a new urban identity. The Cascade Locks were designated in 1992 by the US Department of the Interior as a significant historic district and listed on the National Register of Historic Places. The district is undergoing development as a new addition to Cascade Valley Metro Park. The 8/10-mile Cascade Locks Trail along part of the canal was completed by the state in 1993. The remains of a burgeoning industrial valley can be seen along the path:

the canal and locks, the bygone millrace, a canal-era store and house, and old brick factory buildings.

Those with a taste for adventure can push north of the district to explore the ruins of other canal structures and the seminatural areas along the Little Cuyahoga River. Exercise caution when following rough, informal paths or when bushwhacking. The city is planning to construct a hike-bike trail that follows the former towpath. Contact the Cascade Locks Park Association, 234 Ferndale St., Akron, OH 44304 (216-535-4793) for the latest information.

## Access

Head north from downtown Akron on North Main Street. After 0.1 mile, the street crosses Martin Luther King Jr. Boulevard and becomes North Howard Street. Descend 0.3 mile into the Little Cuyahoga River valley and turn left at the traffic signal at the foot of the hill. You are now on West North Street. Go only 0.1 mile, cross the Ohio & Erie Canal, and turn right onto Ferndale Street. The street opens into the parking lot of the Faith Tabernacle, where you can leave your car. The church is in the center of the historic district.

## Trail

The present footpath extends both south and north from the church parking lot. First walk south and then return to this spot to explore the area to the north. Walk back along West North Street, over the canal, and cross the street to pick up your wood-chipped trail. Lock 14 is on your right. The area to your left, between the trail and North Howard Street, is the site of Cascade Grist Mill, now marked by a copse of cottonwood, mulberry, box-elder, and ash. The mill was built in 1876 by Akron oatmeal entrepreneur Ferdinand Schumacher, who expanded on an earlier mill built in 1840 by William Mitchell. No above-ground evidence remains, but local stories persist that the mill's fabled 37-ton cast-iron water wheel is buried on the site. Schumacher closed Cascade Mill when water power became obsolete and mills no longer needed falling water for their power. He moved to downtown Akron, where he established another company called Quaker Oats.

Pass under the high Cuyahoga Valley Scenic Railroad trestle

*Lock 14 on the old Ohio & Erie Canal*

that spans lock 13 on the canal. Lock 12 is about 200 feet farther up the trail and is visible as you climb steps to come out into the service yard at the loading docks of Ace Rubber Products. Ace Rubber is one of the few working rubber mills remaining in the city once known as the "Rubber Capital of the World." Before decentralization of the rubber industry, nearly three-quarters of the rubber grown in the world was shipped to Akron to be processed. The big rubber companies began to close their Akron production facilities in the 1970s. Now only small companies like Ace Rubber Products, which makes floor mats, are left to carry on the local tradition. The Ace Rubber buildings date from as early as 1910 and are built on the site of the Aetna Mills of 1843. Ace Rubber chose the location mainly because it offered "hydraulic power and cheap transportation by way of the Ohio Canal," according to a 1912 account in *The India Rubber World,* a trade journal.

Just beyond Ace Rubber, note the screened enclosure on the left—a visible remnant of the old millrace. The screen house covers the tunnel intakes that carry the water beneath the Ace Rubber plant. Walk under the Wheeling and Lake Erie Railroad bridge and reach lock 11. Beyond the lock, the drainageway that once was the hydraulic can be seen downslope to your left as you cross a wood bridge.

At the top of the stairs you come upon the Beech Street Steam Plant, marked by three tall steel smokestacks. The plant was built in 1927 by the Akron Steam Heating Company to produce steam heat for downtown buildings. Akron Steam Heating merged with four other firms in 1930 to form the Ohio Edison Company, which continued to produce steam at the facility until 1980. The plant could not survive the spiraling decline of Akron during the 1970s, when the rubber companies moved out and the downtown area decayed. The massive structure is currently abandoned and in disrepair. Ohio Edison still operates the Beech Substation on the canal side.

A wooden viewing platform is above lock 10, the southernmost of the Cascade Locks. Shortly beyond, your trail ends at a large tunnel that bores under Martin Luther King Jr. Boulevard. Urban development sent the canal underground in the city's central business district. Plans call for rescuing the buried canal and restoring it as a testimony to Akron's transportation and industrial heritage.

Walk back to the Faith Tabernacle. Continue north a short distance on Ferndale Street to lock 15 and the Mustill historic area. The Mustill Store fronts the lock and the white-frame Mustill House sits on a low knoll back from the canal. Fred Mustill operated the store as a "swilling place" to serve the needs of canal travelers. The store and house were built about 1853 and are among the oldest structures in Akron. The buildings will be renovated to serve as the centerpiece of the new park.

Cascade Locks Trail ends at the Mustill complex but you can pick your way north along a narrow path to the place where the canal flows into the Little Cuyahoga River at a wide shoal. Lilac bushes and crumbling stone foundations mark old homesites along the path, which once was the northward extension of Ferndale Street.

The trail overlooks the place where the canal burst out of its channel by cutting through the towpath to join the swollen Little Cuyahoga during the great flood of 1913. The flood was the worst ever recorded in Ohio. During Easter week, the entire state was saturated with 4 to 11 inches of rain. Water carried away 20,000 structures, left 200,000 homeless, and killed 467; many of the missing never were found. Damage was estimated at $143 million (about $1.5–2 billion in today's money). In Akron, the situation at Cascade Locks was alarming. The locks, even when their gates were fully open, served to impede the flow of water. In an effort to move the flood downstream even faster, workers dynamited the locks. The rushing water wiped out almost everything in its path as far downstream as Brecksville. Blown up and decimated in the Western Reserve, and destroyed as well over much of the state, the canal never reopened.

A rough trail continues along the river and comes out on unpaved Putnam Street. The street generally follows the former towpath. A short distance ahead on your left lie the ruins of lock 16, the northernmost of the seven Cascade Locks.

The venturesome hiker can push even farther north by bushwhacking straight where Putnam Street curves left to a small residential area. The way near the street is overgrown with Japanese knotweed in summer, but you will eventually scramble out of the thicket and be able to discern the canal prism and the towpath mound. The canal follows the Little Cuyahoga downstream to the Cuyahoga. Here the jarring noise of the city seems far away. This serene piece of forest is alive with the soft sound of moving water and the chamber music of birdsong. Old cottonwoods are full of wrens and mourning doves. Thrushes call from the underbrush, cardinals fly back and forth, swallows snatch flying insects above the water, and orioles build their hanging nests high in the giant sycamores whose branches overhang the river.

Walk as far north as you wish. This faint trail provided far more than just the transport of grain and coal. It was the lifeline of the area. You may find locks 17 and 18 in tangles of briars and vines. Beyond them lies Memorial Parkway, the first highway bridge across the Little Cuyahoga north of Cascade Locks, about 1 mile from West North Street. When ready, turn and retrace your way to the Faith Tabernacle. Cascade Locks Historic District is an enthralling piece of history and nature preserved in the heart of Akron, my hometown.

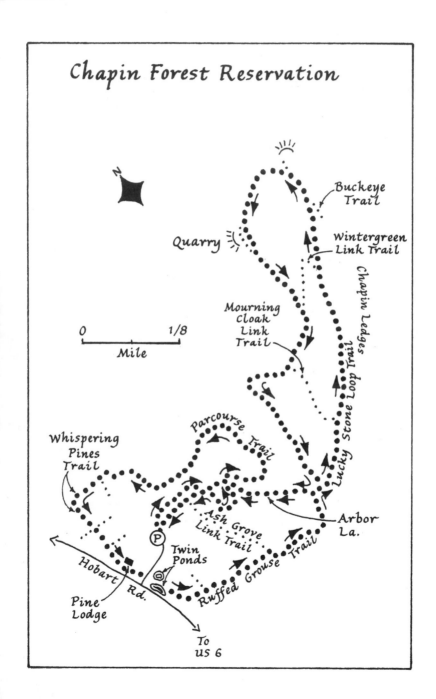

# Chapin Forest
# Reservation

## A scenic hike through Mormon country

*Hiking distance: 4 miles*
*Hiking time: 2 hours*
*Maps: USGS Chesterland; reservation map;*
*Buckeye Trail, Chapin Forest section*

The Western Reserve was fertile ground in the early 1800s for a blossoming of religious fervor. Pioneer Ohio was an open society, relatively free from the traditional constraints of the East Coast, and ripe for the acceptance of new ideas. Some Yankees who felt smothered by church authority immigrated to the Reserve to escape the payment of church taxes, which were collected in New England until the 1820s. In Ohio, religious leaders found that good land was still available at reasonable prices. This receptive atmosphere attracted new religious persuasions.

The Shakers (the United Society of Believers in Christ's Second Appearing) established strong communities at North Union (today's Shaker Heights) and elsewhere in the state. Congregationalists were active in establishing utopian societies by creating towns that would function as Christian communities. Berea, Oberlin, and Tallmadge were bastions of Congregationalism and sources of support for social reform movements. Sandusky and two other Ohio towns were started by James Kilbourne, an Episcopalian priest.

Ohio was directly on the line of the western movement. The Western Reserve was the scene of a major chapter in the Mormons' long journey from New York that ultimately would lead some to the State of Deseret (modern Utah). The Mormons (Church of Jesus Christ of Latter-day Saints) were invited to Ohio by Sidney Rigdon of Kirtland. Rigdon was a former Baptist minister who first converted to the Disciples of Christ and then to Mormonism. Most of his

*Chapin Forest Reservation, a 390-acre gift from Frederic H. Chapin in 1949*

parishioners followed him into the movement. Rigdon traveled to New York in 1830 to visit Joseph Smith Jr., the founder of the new faith. In 1831, Rigdon returned to Kirtland, bringing with him Smith and his wife, Emma. By the end of 1832, area membership in the Mormon Church was estimated as high as 500, consisting of Ohio converts and recently arrived New Yorkers. About this time, Smith received a vision for the construction of a great tabernacle.

Planning and construction of the new church started immediately. The planning committee—Smith, Rigdon, and Frederick G. Williams—decided to use materials native to Lake County: tulip tree, oak, and walnut from the verdant forests and brick from the clays of the Chagrin River. However, the bricks proved too soft, so the committee switched to local sandstone cut from nearby outcroppings south of the building site. Actual construction began on June 5, 1833, when the first wagon of sandstone was unloaded and the foundation was laid. Smith himself served as supervisor at the quarry throughout construction. The building was completed in less than three years— the first temple for the new religion.

Joseph Smith wrote that he had received a revelation from God to move his flock to Ohio: "And there ye might escape the power of the enemy . . . for this cause I gave unto you the commandment, that you should go to . . . Ohio; and there I will give unto you my law."

But the Kirtland Mormons continued to be harassed by "the enemy." At night, non-Mormons ravaged the temple's work site and tore down the walls. Smith was forced to mount armed guards around the building at all times. After construction, the non-Mormons became increasingly hostile. The church's communal land-holding practices alienated some; rumors of nontraditional sexual conduct irritated others. The failure of the Mormon "Anti-Bank of Kirtland" was seen as an injustice by local investors. By 1838, most Mormons had followed Joseph Smith west to Missouri, still searching for the promised land. The small Mormon remnant in Ohio became known as the Reorganized Church of Jesus Christ of Latter Day Saints.

The grand temple and the old quarry can still be seen—enduring monuments to the faith of a people and the history of a place. They speak clearly of an age now gone, palpable evidence of pioneer roots. Today's hike in Chapin Forest Reservation enables you to witness connections between the distant past and the busy present, to trace the ground trod by Smith and his followers through majestic forests of tulip tree and oak and along the ledges, outcrops, and quarries of 300-million-year-old sandstone bedrock.

## Access

Chapin Forest Reservation is located in Kirtland and is one of the Lake Metroparks. Head west on US 6 and turn right on Hobart Road, 1.1 miles from the junction of US 6 and OH 306. Drive for 0.3 mile along Hobart Road and turn right into the reservation. Follow the short entrance road to the parking area and park your car toward the left end. The reservation's trail network begins in the northeastern corner.

## Trail

Start on the Parcourse Trail, a physical fitness trail designed to let you walk or jog between exercise stations set up in the forest using rustic equipment. Cross Arbor Lane, your return loop, twice (once after station 3 and again after station 7) and continue on the Parcourse Trail. The way leads through a mature forest of tulip tree, northern red oak, American beech, sugar maple, and shagbark hickory.

After station 8, the path goes uphill and then turns left to pass near the bottom of a high rock outcropping. The cliffs are composed of a sandstone called Sharon Conglomerate, a distinctive and attractive rock that combines white quartz pebbles and sand grains cemented more or less firmly together. Weathering of exposed conglomerate over the eons has loosened the pearly quartz, resulting in a bountiful supply of pebbles and cobbles scattered on the ground. Ohioans believe the small rocks bring good fortune and call them "lucky stones."

The trail turns left, away from the rocks, and descends to a low clearing. Wet-loving plants like orange touch-me-not and sensitive fern grow profusely in the filtered sunlight. Beyond the opening, the path makes a broad S-turn and reaches station 19. There, turn right on the Whispering Pines Trail.

Walk through the shade of evergreen trees, with northern white cedar on your right and spruce on your left. Small beech and sassafras saplings struggle upward in an effort to pierce the dark canopy. Shortly, your path turns sharply left in a white pine grove. More evergreens (spruce and Scots pine) shade the trail as you walk in turn past a cross trail and then a side trial to your left. Come out into an open area and walk past Pine Lodge, keeping the building on your left. The lodge serves as a nature education center in summer and a cross-country ski center in winter. A telephone, rest rooms, and drinking water are here. The trailhead parking lot is visible to your left.

Continue straight across the park entrance road to Twin Ponds. The first small pond is on your left and a second, larger pond soon comes into view on your right. The sunny ponds are ringed with cattails and rushes. Lake Metroparks stocks them with largemouth bass and channel catfish, so they are popular fishing spots, both for herons and for people. A pair of Canada geese usually rear a brood on the ponds each spring. Pick up your continuing trail just beyond the second pond where a narrow path leaves the grassy area and enters the woods.

Walk through a stand of spruce and cedar, then enter a second-growth deciduous forest. The way curves left and comes out into an opening behind an earthen ramp used as a practice ski slope. A turn to the left here leads back to the developed areas of the park, but you should turn right into the woods on a gravel path—the Ruffed Grouse Trail.

Climb gradually to a T-intersection and turn right, staying on the Ruffed Grouse Trail. Continue uphill to another T-intersection near the base of a rock outcrop. Turn right again; the way is now on Arbor Lane. Veer right at the first opportunity on the Lucky Stone Loop Trail. Watch for the charmed creamy quartz pebbles on and beside this path.

Pass the Mourning Cloak Link Trail on your left and reach the top of the ridge. Your trail is canopied by big, tall trees. Deep cracks and fissures in the earth on the right side of the path indicate the beginning of the spectacular Chapin Ledges. Signs here ask the hiker to stay on the main trail that runs along the top. Entry into the ledges is allowed only with a park guide; scheduled ledges hikes are held twice monthly. The cool, moist environment of the Sharon Conglomerate cliffs provide conditions favored by eastern hemlock. Their light green, feathery needles stand in marked contrast to the broad-leaved hardwoods. Beechdrop, squawroot, and a variety of ferns can be found on the ground.

Pass the Wintergreen Link Trail on your left and then join with the blue-blazed Buckeye Trail as it comes up from your right. Continue straight on the Lucky Stone Loop and Buckeye Trails. Where your path goes left, a short spur continues straight to a rock overlook that offers views of the park during the leafless seasons. Back on the main trail, better vistas are available farther along where a narrow path leads right to a fenced overlook at the top of an abandoned sandstone quarry. The deep quarry before you is a 20th-century operation that closed in the early 1970s. The Mormons' 19th-century diggings are much smaller and are found near the reservation's eastern border, off your trail.

Sweeping views from the cliff reach north to the open waters of Lake Erie. A few structures can be seen, but mostly the landscape is forests or fields. On a clear day, the skyscrapers of downtown Cleveland rise above the northwest horizon, more than 18 miles away.

Follow the cliff path and soon return to the main trail, where you turn right to continue your walk. Pass the Wintergreen and Mourning Cloak Link Trails on your left and come upon a major trail intersection. Turn right; you are now back on Arbor Lane.

Walk past the Ruffed Grouse Trail on your left, the two crossings of the Parcourse Trail, and the Ash Grove Link Trail on your left near a ball field. Your way leads straight to the parking lot.

# Girdled Road Reservation

## A quiet walk in the Big Creek valley

*Hiking distance: 4¾ miles*
*Hiking time: 3 hours*
*Maps: USGS Painesville; reservation map;*
*Buckeye Trail, Burton section*

*[The valley is] where we can still do such a simple thing as walk along a trail and perhaps decide to stand still and be quiet for a while. And standing there, in a place where the only sounds are kinglets overhead, perhaps, or a woodpecker drumming nearby, we can begin to feel reestablished to some degree. This is a priceless gift.*

Professor Tom Lyon writes of another valley far from the Western Reserve, but his words aptly describe this ramble through Girdled Road Reservation. With over 600 acres, the reservation is the largest of the Lake Metroparks. Its size and its relative remoteness in southern Lake County provide a quiet sanctuary for a calming walk in the forest.

This hike consists of both upland and lowland paths. It begins on the rolling plateau, then descends to follow the banks of Big Creek and crosses Aylworth Creek before finally climbing a ragged bluff to return to the heights. Almost all of the trail is canopied by tall hardwoods, with occasional passages through shrubby meadows and small, cool groves of hemlocks. In the valley silver maples, sycamores, tulip trees, and beeches reach out; berries dangle from bushes and dead logs worn smooth by the gentle waters sprawl across the streambed. Cedar waxwings nest in the brush, and graceful belted kingfishers rattle by, occasionally plunging headlong into eddies for minnows and darters.

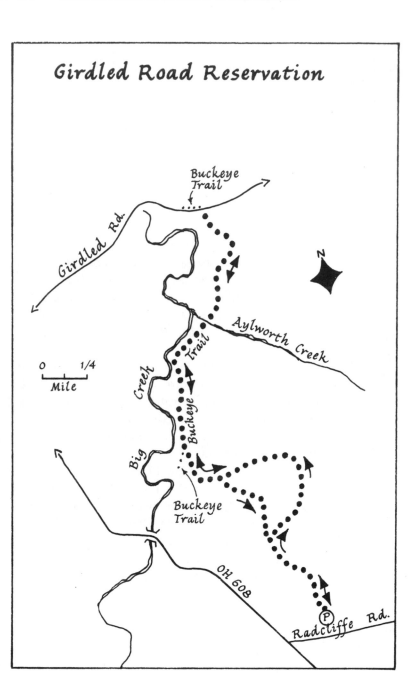

Girdled Road Reservation

The sounds of civilization are distant in the valley. An occasional light plane may pass high above, but mostly you will hear only the soft gurgle of water tumbling over the stones in the stream. Currents of solitude wash down the deep valley, creating a strange privacy that is increasingly rare in our hurried world. Girdled Road Reservation is a good place to walk to recapture the quietness of bygone days.

Girdled Road runs along the northern boundary of the park. It follows the trace of the first road built in the Western Reserve. The approximate route was recommended by surveyors in 1797 as they labored in the wilderness to lay out township boundaries. In 1798, the Connecticut Land Company hired General Simon Perkins to cut a road 25 feet wide and to girdle trees to a width of 35 feet on a long swath extending from the mouth of the Cuyahoga River on Lake Erie to the Pennsylvania border. The road was used by settlers attracted to the new western lands opening up at the end of the 18th century.

Horses use some of the trails, resulting in churned-up, muddy conditions in low areas along the way. Hiking boots are advised.

## Access

Girdled Road Reservation is in Concord and Leroy Townships. From the square in Painesville, head south on Liberty Street, which becomes Ravenna Road outside town. Drive 3.5 miles and turn left on OH 608 (Concord-Hambden Road). Go 3.4 miles to Radcliffe Road at the Geauga County line. Turn left again. The main park entrance is on the left after 0.2 mile. Follow the short entrance road to the back of the parking lot at the edge of the large playing field.

## Trail

The trail entrance, framed by wooden fencing, is at the northeast corner of the playing field. The path crosses old fields and hedgerows, but soon enters a scrubby forest. The park district has placed nest boxes for eastern bluebirds throughout the open areas.

Shortly after reaching the woods, the trail splits. You will return to this place later, but for now fork right on the east trail, which winds through meadows and forests. The two trails come back to-

*One-fourth of Ohio is woodland, including 643-acre Girdled Road Reservation.*

gether just before you begin a curving descent into the Big Creek valley. The creek has carved a fracture in the plateau as it sweeps northward from its headwaters in the highlands near Chardon to its junction with the Grand River south of Painesville.

At the bottom, come upon a T-junction with the Buckeye Trail along Big Creek. Turn right (north) and head downstream. The way threads through the beech and hemlock woods fringing the water, alternating between the high terrace above the stream and the low floodplain along the creek's edge.

Cross Aylworth Creek near where it flows into Big Creek and climb steeply out of the Aylworth gorge. Your path drops in and out of another ravine before reaching the parking lot on Girdled Road.

The Buckeye Trail continues north out of the park on its way to Lake Erie. Turn around and retrace your way to the entrance trail where you first came upon the Buckeye Trail. Climb to near the top of the ridge, then bear right to return along the west trail to the parking lot.

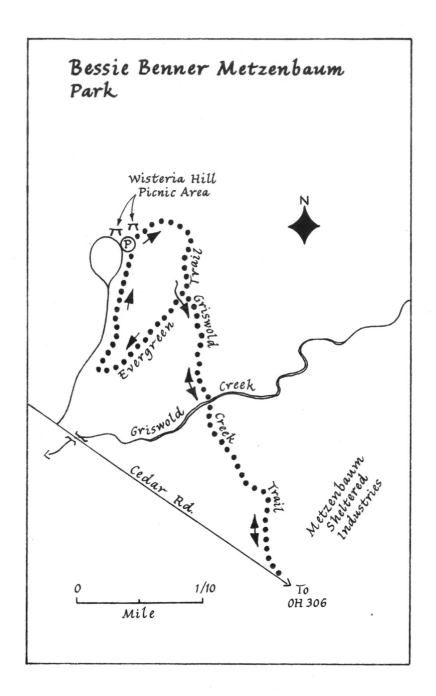

# Bessie Benner Metzenbaum Park

## A wheelchair-accessible trail through woods and swamps

*Hiking distance: ¾ mile*
*Hiking time: ½ hour*
*Maps: USGS Chesterland; park map*

James Metzenbaum, a young Cleveland lawyer, married Bessie Benner on December 31, 1906. They moved into a big house on Euclid Avenue in Euclid. James, although "of small physical build" and "burdened with an ailing body," possessed a "towering intellect" that helped him build a successful law practice. Bessie was described as "a beautiful blonde . . . so stunning in her delicate beauty that people on Euclid Avenue would stop to gaze on her loveliness."

While the couple were on vacation in Florida in 1920, Bessie died suddenly and unexpectedly of unknown causes. James was thrown into profound grief and despair. Returning home to Ohio, he shuttered their home in Euclid and moved into the Statler Hotel in Cleveland. Bessie's remains were cremated and interred at Lake View Cemetery. James had a special mausoleum built, complete with small living quarters with electricity and a rocking chair. There he would go to sit quietly or to read poetry aloud. James battled deep depression for the rest of his life. He plunged into social reform and civic works in search of an anchor and haven. James established himself as a spokesman for many causes, including the feeding of hungry schoolchildren, improved working conditions for teachers, support of libraries, and, most prominently, the promotion of urban planning. Due to the pioneering work of James in Cleveland and Alfred Bettman in Cincinnati, Ohio became America's leader in city planning in the 1920s. In 1926, James successfully argued the constitutionality of Euclid's zoning laws before the US Supreme Court in a landmark case.

*Loma Deremer enjoys the boardwalk over the Griswold Creek bottom land.*

Eventually, his growing stature as a reform activist moved James toward a political goal, election to public office. He served first on the Cleveland School Board and later three terms as state senator. But the haunting memory of Bessie never left him. James often spent sleepless nights on long drives through the countryside. On one such night in the 1940s he discovered an old farm in Chester Township in Geauga County. He was seized with the idea of developing a memorial on the land for his beloved Bessie.

James soon purchased about 100 acres of woods and fields. In 1948 he founded a charitable corporation called the Bessie Benner Metzenbaum Foundation and deeded over 50 acres of land to the new organization. The foundation asserted itself as his dominant interest, and its advancement became his highest priority. James undertook his latest crusade with characteristic fervor. He would arrive at the Chester property at 3 or 4, morning after morning, working on the farm before going to his Cleveland law office by 9 AM. Many evenings were also spent on the project. His plan was to establish a facility for the use of deprived or handicapped children "regardless of race, color or creed, and without cost to such children." The foundation established a school for children and later a sheltered workshop for handicapped adults.

December 31, 1960, was cold and snowy in Cleveland. It was James and Bessie's 54th wedding anniversary. James, now 77, had lived through inconsolable sorrow for over 40 years. While visiting Bessie's grave at Lake View after sundown, he suffered a heart attack in the small mausoleum. James managed to leave the cemetery, but collapsed again on the sidewalk. Rising once more, he reached the front porch of a house on Mayfield Road, where he died.

## Access

Head south from Chardon on OH 44 for 3.3 miles to US 322 (Mayfield Road). Turn right and proceed for 7.3 miles to the junction with OH 306 in Chesterland. Go left on 306, drive for 1.0 mile, and turn right on Cedar Road at the first traffic signal. The entrance to the park is on the right about 0.9 mile from this intersection. Follow the short park road to the end and leave your car at Wisteria Hill Picnic Area.

## Trail

In 1991, the Bessie Benner Metzenbaum Foundation gave 65 acres of land in its southwestern corner to the Geauga Park District. The new park, with Bessie as its eponym, was designed with James's wish to serve "people with a wide variety of interests and abilities." Your trail is accessible by wheelchair users and connects with the foundation grounds to the east. The path passes through a range of wooded habitats—deciduous forest, evergreen forest, and lowland thicket—and offers visitors much diversity in a short distance.

Pick up the paved Evergreen Trail on the right side of the parking lot. The path leads past the rest rooms and under a wisteria arbor before entering the woods. Wisteria was Bessie's favorite flower and a prominent part of the landscaping around the couple's Euclid home. James brought cuttings from Bessie's wisteria vines and planted them all around the Chester property.

Your way winds through a broadleaf forest of big beech trees and smaller sugar maples; wildflowers, especially May-apples, are a highlight of this trail in the spring. The path soon enters a grove of white pines. The evergreens are home to red squirrels, a northern species typical of coniferous forests. Turn left on the paved Griswold Creek Trail.

The path descends slightly and reaches a winding boardwalk that carries you across the creek and its mucky margins. The boardwalk provides outstanding views of the bottomland and its wealth of living things. Plant growth is rampant and chaotic. Birds flit through the thickets and call from the canopy. The stream and its backwater pools harbor small fish, frogs, and turtles. Languid Griswold Creek is here near its headwaters and brings to mind the words of Thoreau: a "little black-veined brook in the midst of the marsh, just beginning to meander, winding slowly round a decaying stump." The creek runs a short southwesterly course and eventually flows into the Chagrin River.

The trail leaves the boardwalk and reenters a coniferous woods before ending at Metzenbaum Sheltered Industries, Inc. Retrace your way back to the Evergreen Trail and there turn left. Your path leads through a mixed forest of conifers and hardwoods before it curves right and climbs gradually to near the park road. Continue to Wisteria Hill Picnic Area.

# Punderson
# State Park

### An exceptional area with dramatic, glacially influenced topography

*Hiking distance: 7¼ miles*
*Hiking time: 3½ hours*
*Maps: USGS Burton; park map*

T his figure-8 hike explores most of Punderson State Park, a 1000-acre park that, with its surrounding area, is a huge glacial deposit of till (sand, gravel, rocks, and boulders), moraines, and kames assembled during the last Ice Age. The resulting glacial geology is fascinating and famous, as are the natural habitats it has produced: the lakes and swamps nestled in deep forests, botanical habitats, and accompanying animal communities.

About 50,000 years ago, the Earth's climate again became so cool and moist that more snow fell in northern lands than could melt in succeeding summers, so sheets of ice gradually accumulated. These moved slowly southward, grinding off vast amounts of soil and rock on the way—"God's plow" is how John Muir described the glacier. This immense continental ice sheet, designated the "Wisconsinan" after the state where it has been most thoroughly studied, continued to build for more than 35,000 years. Most of midland North America and all of what became the Western Reserve were completely covered by mountains of ice.

Approximately 12,000–14,000 years ago, the Earth's climate began to get warmer and drier. The Great Ice began a slow retreat to the polar region, leaving behind a land vastly different from before. Topography was altered, stream systems were modified, and lakes—which Henry David Thoreau called "the landscape's most beautiful and expressive feature"—were created. At the time the glaciers were receding from Ohio, large blocks of ice broke off from the main mass.

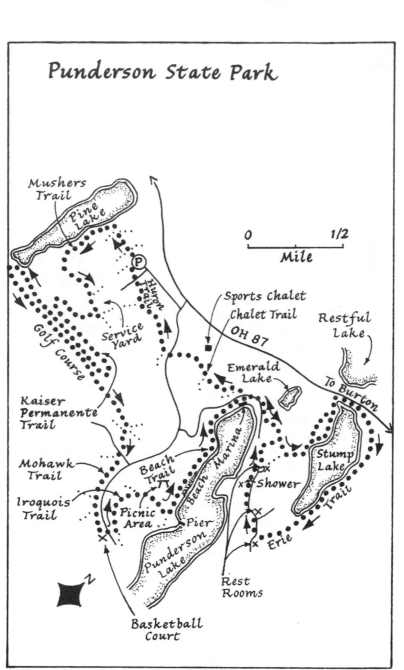

Punderson State Park

Mushers Trail

Pine Lake

P

Huron Trail

Service Yard

Golf Course

Sports Chalet
Chalet Trail
OH 87

Restful Lake

Emerald Lake

To Burton

0      1/2
Mile

Kaiser Permanente Trail

Mohawk Trail

Iroquois Trail

Beach Trail

Beach Marina

Stump Lake

Erie Trail

Shower

Picnic Area

Pier

Punderson Lake

Rest Rooms

N

Basketball Court

*Early evening scene of Stump Lake along the Erie Trail*

Great quantities of meltwater flowing past the blocks deposited clay and gravel and buried them. Over time, the ice blocks melted, leaving the lake beds filled with water. These are called kettle hole or pothole lakes. Some of the ice-carved kettle holes are huge. Punderson Lake, the largest and deepest natural lake wholly in Ohio, covers over 100 acres and is more than 60 feet deep. It is also one of the clearest and coldest, with a sandy bottom largely covered with muck and decaying vegetation.

Surrounding the kettles are kames—irregular, well-developed knobs or hummocks that rise 70 to 80 feet above lake level. The large tract of numerous wooded kames in Punderson State Park is one of the best preserved sections of the Kent Moraine, a broad belt of hummocky topography stretching from Stark County to northwestern Pennsylvania. The Kent Moraine is about 5 miles wide in the Punderson area. The impressive knob-and-kettle topography of south-central Geauga County was studied by pioneer geologist Charles Whittlesey, who published his findings in 1838.

Ohio has 27 natural lakes, all in the glaciated portion of the state. Three of them—Punderson, Emerald, and Restful—can be seen on this hike, along with two artificial lakes (Pine and Stump).

Some of the trails described here are used by skiers, dogsledders, and snowmobilers in winter. Punderson State Park recently changed the names of many of its trails. Some old maps still use the former names. The names in this chapter match those on signs and on new park maps. Many sections of the trail are wet and muddy most of the year. Mosquitoes and deerflies are common. Part of the hike is on the park's nature trail, with numbered stations along the way described in a pamphlet available at park headquarters or the lodge.

## Access

Drive west from the square in Burton on OH 87. After 4.2 miles, turn left into Punderson State Park. Go just a short distance and take the first road to your right. Go 0.2 mile to the end of the road and leave your car in the Pine Lake parking lot, which serves as the trailhead for the park's network of cross-country ski and dogsled trails.

## Trail

Walk west on the Mushers Trail. Keep straight through an old field, ignoring broad trails that go left and right, and enter the woods. Descend rather steeply to Pine Lake. The impoundment, sometimes called Green Pine Lake, is the first of the five lakes and reservoirs you will see on today's hike. At the water, turn left and follow the shoreline south. The trail eventually curves left, away from the lake, and climbs back into a moist, shrubby old field. The fields are ideal mating grounds for American woodcocks. Male birds can be seen performing their spectacular aerial courtship displays at dusk in April and May.

Turn right at a T-intersection. The trail skirts the park service building and yard on your left. At the far corner of the fenced yard, turn right off the Mushers Trail and enter the forest on a very short connector trail. Turn right again in a few feet; you are now on the broad Kaiser Permanente Trail, sometimes simply called the Kaiser Trail. You are walking on till, a blanket of unsorted earth, rubble, rocks, gravel, and sand deposited by the glacier. The till in this area is up to 150 feet deep; this may have been a former valley now buried with drift. The kames you will climb later in the hike are also veneered with till, although the drift tends to be thinner on the knobs. The occasional boulders, called erratics, you see in the woods are chunks of Canadian granite sheared off by the glacier and carried here, where they were dropped in the meltwater.

The Kaiser Permanente Trail is mostly level as it winds through the forest, but there is a gentle descent to near the swampy southern end of Pine Lake before you climb to a long straightaway that skirts the Punderson Golf Course on your right.

At a cross trail, turn right on a wide connecting path, leaving the Kaiser Permanente Trail. Come to a side trail that leads right to the golf course, but your path curves left and comes out of the woods at a clearing along a paved road. Walk straight, cross the road, and continue on the Mohawk Trail. Keep left at a fork and pass through a young forest of cottonwood, hawthorns, maples, and Scots pine. The main park road parallels your trail on the left. A side trail leads to the right before you reach a T-intersection in a lowland. Turn left, cross a run on a wood bridge, and climb out of the little valley. The Mohawk Trail ends after 6/10 mile as you come out of the woods at a basketball court, part of the recreational complex that surrounds Manor House, the park's lodge.

Veer left, keeping the court on your right, cross the road and a parking lot, and reenter the woods. The Iroquois Trail, the park's interpretative trail, runs along the back of the parking area. Turn left and descend; you will soon come upon station 10 along the trail. You walk past descending stations (9, 8, 7, etc.). Beyond a side trail to the left, you come out into the picnic area.

Turn right and follow a gravel lane along the edge of the picnic grounds. The lane continues to a headland above Punderson Lake. A small fishing pier juts into the water and the Iroquois Trial curves right. The lake has good stands of submerged aquatic plants (including chara, coontail, and pondweeds) and floating spatterdock and water-lilies. Fish are never particularly diverse in glacial lakes, but a 1987 survey of Punderson netted a good variety of species that depend on clear, unsilted, unpolluted water, including grass pickerel, lake chub, emerald shiner, sand shiner, largemouth bass, yellow bullhead, black bullhead, white crappie, bluegill, warmouth, and pump-kinseed, in addition to the ubiquitous common carp. Because of its cool water temperature, Punderson Lake has been stocked by the state with rainbow and golden trout, two species from the western United States. Despite its pristine appearance, Punderson faces some disturbing problems. Heavy algal growth may indicate sewage or other runoff from the state park facilities. The state has started a $400,000 upgrade of the wastewater and sewage collection systems as a result of a bond issue passed by Ohio voters in 1993.

Turn left on a path that leads along the shore to the swimming beach. Walk across the 600-foot beach or along the walkway at the back and continue along the shore path (the Beach Trail) through the woods on the far side.

The trail leads in 4/10 mile to a small marina. Several picnic tables are here, along with rest rooms. The marina is at the center of the figure-8 of this hike. To continue with the second loop, walk past the boathouse/camp store and parking lot and turn right on the road. Walk a short distance along the road as it crosses a low area, then turn left on the 2¼-mile Erie Trail.

Curve right up a kame as you climb gradually. Another gift of the glacier shimmers below and to the left—Emerald Lake, an oval kettle lake surrounded by a swamp thicket. Come to a fork in the trail. You will return to this spot later, but for now keep left and walk downhill. Reach a small pond where a side trail comes down from your right. Turn left and cross a low dam, keeping the woodland pond on your right.

The Erie Trail splits in the vicinity of Stump Lake, with the right fork staying close to the water and the left prong following a more upland route. The two segments rejoin later. Circle around Stump Lake, keeping the lake on your right. At the north end, your trail follows the narrow dike separating the lake from OH 87. Visible to the north across the highway and outside the park is Restful Lake, the third glacial pothole on today's hike.

The path curves around Stump Lake and leads south along the lake's eastern shore. The swampy southern end of Stump Lake is a favored nesting site for Canada geese and wood ducks. The trail leaves the lake behind and leads through an upland forest on a cluster of kames before reaching the campground. The Erie Trail comes out behind a rest room; turn right on the campground road. The park's camping area is built on numerous kames. Walk uphill, keeping left where another road goes right. Pass a rest room on your right where a loop road goes left. Turn right at the next road, just past campsite 158 on your right. Pass a shower house on the left and reach the end of the road. Keep left on the cul-de-sac and pick up your trail as it enters the woods to the right of campsite 190.

Your path descends to the fork on the Erie Trail mentioned above. Rejoin the Erie Trail and walk back to the marina. Just past the marina, follow the 3/10-mile Chalet Trail to the sports chalet as it leaves a parking lot on the right side of the road. Walk uphill on another kame on a broad path through a scrubby forest. Keep right at a fork, pass a side trail to your left, and come out at three lighted tennis courts, part of the chalet's recreational web.

Keep the courts and the chalet on your right and walk through a small picnic area set in a pine grove. Skirt a parking lot by keeping to the left and reenter the woods on a broad trail. Cross the main park road, enter the forest, and very shortly come to a T-intersection; turn right on the broad Huron Trail.

In an opening, a side trail comes in from your left. Stay straight and cross a road. At the next cross trail, turn right to the Pine Lake parking lot.

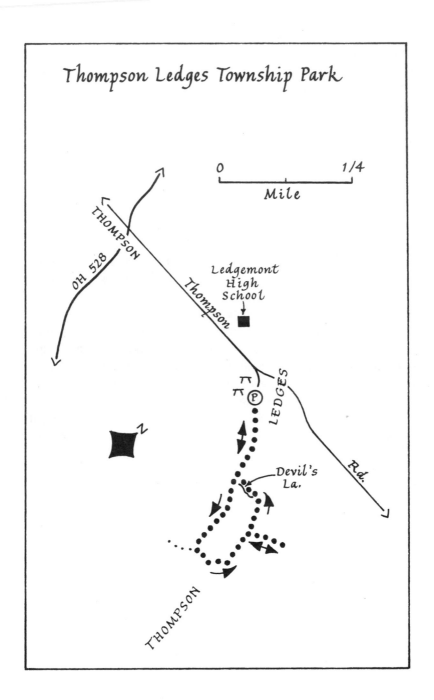

# Thompson Ledges Township Park

0        1/4

Mile

THOMPSON

OH 528

Thompson

Ledgemont
High
School

LEDGES

Rd.

Ⓟ

Devil's
La.

N

THOMPSON

# Thompson Ledges
# Township Park
### Rambling on Paleozoic bedrock

*Hiking distance: ¾ mile*
*Hiking time: 45 minutes*
*Map: USGS Thompson*

Among the most prominent features of the landscape in the Western Reserve are sandstone cliffs, known as "ledges" in Northeast Ohio. Ledges occur sporadically as outliers or caprock in isolated areas on the Allegheny Plateau. This hike explores the northernmost outcrop, a striking geologic landmark called Thompson Ledges, protected since 1937 by Thompson Township.

Thompson Ledges are composed of Sharon Conglomerate, a pebbly sandstone of the Pennsylvanian Period. Sharon Conglomerate is the youngest bedrock formation in the Western Reserve, having been deposited about 300 million years ago. The attractive sedimentary rock is composed of fine grains of sand cemented together and holding characteristic rounded, white quartz pebbles. The crystalline pebbles were washed down from the north in great, ancient rivers after being eroded from igneous rocks of the Canadian Shield. When the rivers reached the flatlands of Ohio, they fanned out and formed a vast network of braiding and crisscrossing channels. The loads of pebbles and sand dropped out in the slow-flowing water. Gradually, over unimaginable eons, the layers of sediment and pebbles solidified into layers of sandstone.

The ledges are home to unusual plants that often are uncommon elsewhere in the area. Mosses and lichens are plentiful and many ferns find their specific ecological niches among the rocks. Look for bracken, sensitive fern, woodferns, hayscented fern, cinnamon fern, common polypody, and interrupted fern.

## Access

Thompson Ledges Township Park is in Geauga County about a quarter mile east of Thompson on the south side of Thompson Road, opposite Ledgemont High School. Enter on the short, single-lane, dirt entrance road and park under the trees. Picnic tables, a picnic shelter, a small playground, rest rooms, and drinking water are here.

## Trail

Follow the narrow gravel road that leads from the parking area along the top of the ledges. Make your way through a gate and pass a tennis court on your right. A trail leads left here to where Devil's Lane, a narrow fissure, cuts through the rock. You will return to this spot later, but for now keep straight on the road.

The top of the outcrop tends to be dry because Sharon Conglomerate is a porous rock. Snowmelt and rain are absorbed by the loose-grained sandstone and carried downward. The plant community on top of the ledges is mostly composed of species like chestnut oak, blueberry, huckleberry, and others that can tolerate relatively low moisture conditions. Erosion has loosened countless quartz pebbles, which are scattered all about. They are known here and elsewhere in the Western Reserve as "lucky stones."

An overlook offers long-ranging views from the east-facing outcrop into the Grand River valley and the folds of ridges beyond that roll into Pennsylvania. The Grand River, hidden by trees, curls through the broad valley about 8 miles from the ledges.

Where the lane curves right, go left and descend along a break in the rock face to the bottom of the cliff. Settling of the massive sandstone over geologic time has caused narrow cracks and chasms to develop.

Turn left and walk along the foot of the ledges. The environment at the bottom is much wetter and cooler than at the top. The plant community here is very different from the one above, characterized by moisture- or cool-loving species such as eastern hemlock, yellow birch, Canada yew, and common spicebush. Water percolates down through the sandstone until it meets the impervious siltstone of the Sharpsville Formation that underlies Thompson Ledges. There it

*Naturalist Judy Barnhart leads a hike at Thompson Ledges. (Beverly J. Brown)*

exits the cliff face in seeps and springs. Yellowish-orange colors on the rock show where iron is precipitating out. The siltstone is of the Mississippian Period, at least 30 million years older than the Sharon Conglomerate sandstone. Both siltstone and sandstone were laid down during the Paleozoic Era, a 375-million-year span dominated by invertebrates and marked by the origin of fish, amphibians, reptiles, and land plants. Because it is soft and easily eroded, the siltstone provides an unstable base for the heavy sandstone. Massive chunks of rock slip and break off at the edge of the ledges.

Turn right on a faint trail and descend a short distance to a pipe spring near a dirt road that runs to a lower picnic area. Return to the trail along the bottom of the cliff and turn right.

Soon reach Devil's Lane, the narrow passageway that leads up through the ledges; turn left. Steps cut into the rock underfoot help you climb. The crevasse is about 3 feet wide at the bottom, but narrows as you reach the top. The rock in the fracture is moist, a sign of the water that is always seeping through the sandstone. On hot summer days the cleft is remarkably cooler than the surroundings. Damp-loving crane flies hover and flit about. Look closely for the cross-veining in the rock formation, evidence of the flow of the old rivers that brought this material from the north. Come out near the tennis court and turn right to reach the parking area.

# Aurora Sanctuary

## A pleasant forest walk, with a river, a creek, wetlands, and ponds

*Hiking distance: 2 miles*
*Hiking time: 1 hour*
*Maps: USGS Aurora; sanctuary map*

The 161-acre Aurora Sanctuary is one of two preserves in Aurora owned by the Audubon Society of Greater Cleveland, a chapter of the National Audubon Society. The Aurora Sanctuary protects a wide variety of habitats, including forested wetlands, swamps, ponds, upland woods, and bottomland forests. The Aurora Branch of the Chagrin River flows through the preserve. The diverse ecosystems support large populations of resident and migrant birds, as well as a host of many other animals and plants.

This hike mostly follows the sanctuary's interpretative trail. Numbered signs along the way identify trees and other natural and historic features. A pamphlet, including a map, is available from the Audubon Society of Greater Cleveland, 140 Public Square, Cleveland, OH 44114 (216-861-5093). Boardwalks and other improvements lift the trail above low areas, but much of the path remains muddy during most of the year; waterproof boots are recommended in wet seasons.

## Access

From the center of Aurora, drive east on East Pioneer Trail for 1.8 miles to the sanctuary. A small parking lot, marked by a sign reading "Audubon Sanctuary Parking," is on your right, 0.2 mile beyond the intersection with North Page Road.

## Trail

Walk west on a mowed swath that runs between an old field and a hedgerow along East Pioneer Trail. Turn right through a break in the

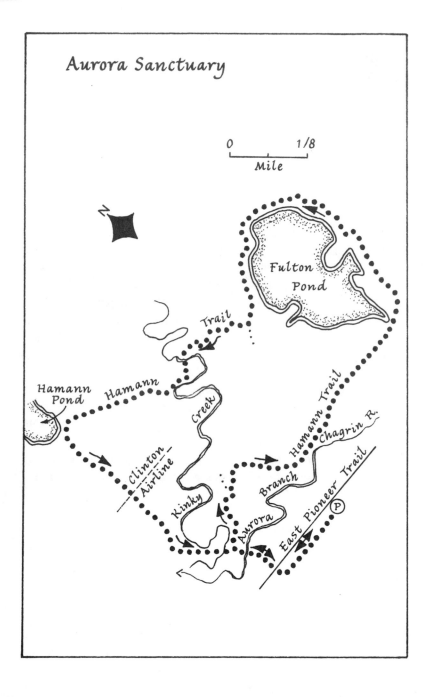

hedgerow, cross the road, and enter the woods on a broad trail. The way descends to the Aurora Branch of the Chagrin River on old Crooks Road. The abandoned right-of-way is often muddy; an alternate footpath keeps to the high ground to the left of the road.

Cross the branch on a wood footbridge supported by sandstone abutments that once anchored the road span. The old highway bridge was washed away in the big flood of 1913. Reach a small bulletin board and a sign announcing the entrance to the sanctuary. You will return to this spot later; for now, turn right on a narrow footpath, the Hamann Trail. The trail is named for Carl Hamann, a founding member of the Audubon Society of Greater Cleveland.

Follow the Hamann Trail, usually marked by red horizontal paint blazes on trees, as it climbs steps and passes through a thickset second-growth forest. Keep straight where the White Trail goes left. The way enters a more mature forest, then drops slightly to skirt an arm of Fulton Pond on your left. The Hamann Trail circles the pond and breaks out of the forest to cross a wetland on a boardwalk below the dam. The low area is flecked with alders, common elderberry, European buckthorn, silky dogwood, steeplebush spirea, rice cut grass, boneset, tall ironweed, jewelweeds, and sensitive fern. Climb to higher ground as the path loops to an overlook of Fulton Pond. The trail passes through thickets surrounding the pond, descends to another boardwalk, then climbs slightly to return to the upland forest.

Pass White Trail on your left. Descend along an old road cut to cross a stream (called Kinky Creek because of its meanders). Farther along, the path comes out of the woods into a grassy meadow surrounding Hamann Pond. Turn left and follow the way through a thick stand of reed canary grass.

Reenter the forest. The trail uses steps and a boardwalk to cross the old Clinton Airline, a railroad grade dating from the 1850s. The inspiration of Henry Noble Day of Hudson, the railroad was to stretch from New York City to Council Bluffs on the Missouri River. Day named the enterprise after former Governor DeWitt Clinton of New York, a champion of western expansion; "airline" referred to the railroad's direct grade, bridging ravines on high trestles and burrowing through mountains with long tunnels. The soaring cost of con-

*Fulton Pond on the Hamann Trail is one of the highlights of Aurora Sanctuary.*

struction, coupled with an economic downturn, caused the Clinton Airline Company to fold in 1856.

The way follows a ridge above Kinky Creek, then angles down to old Crooks Road to cross the stream on a footbridge. Soon reach the edge of the sanctuary. Follow the old roadway to return to the parking lot.

# Tinker's Creek State Park

## A wetlands walk

*Hiking distance: 2 miles*
*Hiking time: 1 hour*
*Maps: USGS Aurora and Twinsburg*

Tinker's Creek State Park protects almost 300 acres of wetlands in the headwaters of Tinkers Creek, the Cuyahoga River's largest tributary. It also preserves the original spelling of the creek, a name given by Moses Cleaveland in memory of Captain Joseph Tinker.

Tinker was chief boatman on Cleaveland's surveying expedition to the Western Reserve in 1796. The group consisted of 50 men and two women. Surveyors in frontier Ohio were required to sign an oath to carry out their responsibilities in an exemplary manner: "You and each of you, do solemnly and sincerely swear in the Presence of almighty god the searcher of all hearts, that you will Faithfully and impartially execute your duties . . . in the Present Survey now to be made . . . according to the best of your Skills, Judgements, & abilities, & this you promise to answer to god at the great day."

Cleaveland's group made good progress, but they were hampered by the trackless wilderness, disease, and inadequate food. By October, their work was still unfinished. With cold weather coming on, Cleaveland and most of his men returned to Connecticut, leaving behind a small overwintering party of 10 men, women, and children.

A new surveying expedition of 63 men, including Joseph Tinker, returned to the Western Reserve in 1797 to finish the work. This group, with a year's experience on the frontier, came better prepared with more provisions, a resupply plan, and a physician. But they were plagued with bad luck. Maxfield Ludlow, a deputy surveyor, wrote of the hardships along the southern boundary of the Western Reserve:

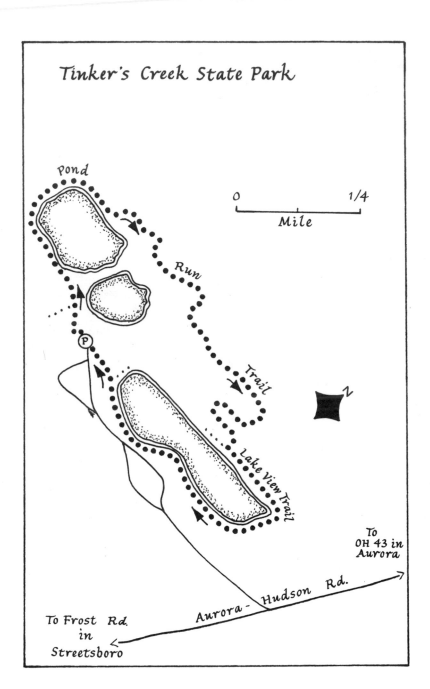

Tinker's Creek State Park

*This flotilla crosses Tinker's Creek State Park's largest pond. (Beverly J. Brown)*

"We here are in danger of our lives . . . I have travelled the woods for 7 years, but never saw so hedious a place as this."

Almost every man in the company was seriously ill with dysentery or fever (likely malaria). Seth Pease, third in command, entered in his diary: "Friday, 7th July—I was so ill as not to be able to assist. In the afternoon after I had traveled 1½ mile I took a dose of Tartar Emetic. This puked me several times. At night I felt some better." One man drowned while attempting to swim his horse across the Grand

River. Another died on the trail with "putrid fever." Two more died of dysentery. A major catastrophe struck when Tinker and two others were lost when their boat capsized during a storm on Lake Erie.

Your hike passes through terrain that made going difficult for the 18th-century surveyors—tangled swamps and quaking mire, with ravenous mosquitoes in summer. Your way is made easier by trail improvements such as ditching, bridging, and boardwalking, but portions of the trail tread are still very wet and muddy. Waterproof boots are recommended. Your trail never reaches Tinkers Creek itself. It remains inaccessible and hidden behind chaotic plant growth in its convoluted channel almost 1 mile to the west.

## Access

Tinker's Creek State Park is in Aurora and Streetsboro. From the center of Aurora, drive south on OH 43 for 0.5 mile and turn right on Aurora-Hudson Road. Go 2.5 miles to the park entrance on your right. Follow the park road 0.4 mile to the farthest parking lot.

From Streetsboro, proceed north on OH 43 for 1.6 miles and turn left on Frost Road. Drive another 1.6 miles and turn right on Aurora-Hudson Road. The park entrance is on your left after 1.3 miles. Follow the above directions to reach the trailhead.

## Trail

About 75 percent of the park is wetlands, mostly swamp forest and swamp thicket populated with beavers, wood ducks, herons, and exquisitely shaped trees. Before stepping off, it is appropriate to re-member the words of Henry David Thoreau: "I enter a swamp as a sacred place. There is the strength, the marrow of Nature."

The wood-chipped Pond Run Trail begins at the far side of the parking area on a broad swath through scrub-shrub wetlands. Short paths lead right to two ponds that are mostly ringed with cattails. Keep straight where the Gentian Trail comes in from the left. The trail crosses channels that run from the ponds. A drainageway and forested wetlands are found on the left.

The path circles to the right around the larger pond, then turns left to leave the shore and cross a drainageway on a wooden bridge.

The way weaves through a variety of miniature ecosystems: a swamp forest with lichen-blanketed tree trunks, a thorny brushland, a rock-strewn upland forest with beautiful spring flowers, and rich scrub-shrub wetlands that attract colorful wood warblers.

Climb a low dike to come to a T-intersection with the Lake View Trail, a path that circles the park's 10-acre impoundment. Turn left. Loop around the lake, keeping it on your right. Walk by the playground, picnic area, sand swimming beach, and park office with rest rooms. Where the Lake View Trail curves right to continue along the shore, keep straight to descend off the dike and return to your vehicle.

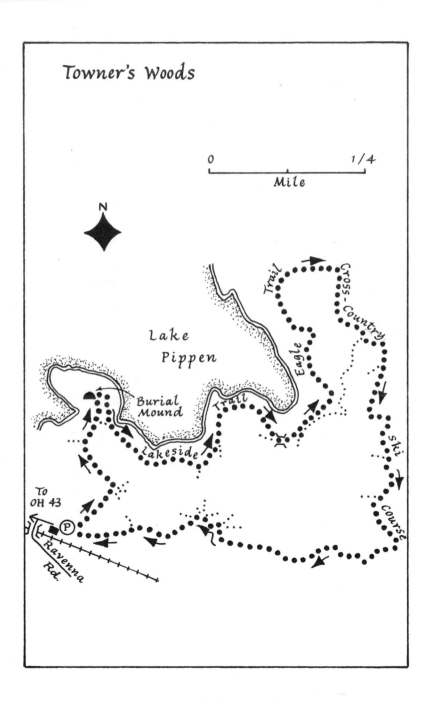

Towner's Woods

0        1/4
Mile

N

Lake
Pippen

Burial
Mound

Lakeside

Trail

Eagle

Trail

Cross-Country

Ski

Course

To
OH 43

Ravenna
Rd.

# Towner's Woods

## Pathways through the sacred ancestral lands of the Hopewell

*Hiking distance: 2¼ miles*
*Hiking time: 1½ hours*
*Map: USGS Kent*

This circuit hike explores the hallowed lands of the ancient Hopewell, a once grand and glorious civilization of the Americas. This outpost of their old empire, in the Cuyahoga Valley on the shores of glacial Lake Pippen, is the location of a lone Hopewell burial mound. The site is protected by Towner's Woods, one of the parks administered by the Portage County Park District.

The Hopewell chose an evocative landscape for the tranquil resting place of 11 of their tribe, probably members of an illustrious caste of rulers or priests and their families or servants. The surrounding forest mantles glacial kames that seem to mimic the mound's conical shape. At the foot of many of the kames nestle impenetrable bogs and tangled vernal pools. The crooked Cuyahoga River once curled through a lush floodplain nearby. The barrow sits on a knoll above the deep, cold waters of Lake Pippen. The lake is unique among all the others in the region. It is a marl lake and its waters are alkaline because the ice sheet left limy rocks and pebbles on the bedrock at the bottom. One cannot help but believe that the Hopewell, who must have been masters of reading the land, regarded this storied place as holy, consecrated by wind and water and sun.

For over a millennium the Towner Mound, as it is now called, lay covered by the verdant forest—"something not known by anyone at all, but wild in our breast for centuries," as poet Anna Akhmatova wrote. An archaeological excavation performed in 1932 revealed 1500-year-old burials. Recent efforts, fueled by a strong private initiative, are aimed at restoring the mound.

Ohio has an exceptionally rich store of Native American culture and sites, especially from the prehistoric period. A gentle, south-facing slope on a gravel kame in Sharon Township, Medina County, is the newly discovered location of the oldest known human-made structure in North America. Recent excavations by an archaeological team from the Cleveland Museum of Natural History found the remnants of a wood shelter constructed around 9000 B.C.—nearly one and a half times as old as any other structure on the continent. The dig, known as the Paleo Crossing Site, also unearthed many chert projectile points, leading to conjecture that the site may have been a hunter's camp.

Millennia passed before the arrival of the Hopewell, one of the most advanced cultures of antiquity. Part of a group of Native Americans known as the Mound Builders, the Hopewell governed a territory centered in the Scioto-Muskingum-Miami river system of southern Ohio, but their culture extended outward to western New York, along the southern shore of Lake Erie into Michigan, and as far west as Iowa and Missouri. Their influence reached even further, as shown by the varied artifacts found in their burial mounds. The Hopewell established a trading network that extended from the Rocky Mountains to the Atlantic Ocean and from north of Lake Superior to the Gulf of Mexico. By a system of water routes and overland trails, the Hopewell traded Ohio flint, pipestone, and fresh-water pearls for silver, obsidian, copper, mica, shark's teeth, and conch shells.

The Hopewell culture may have begun as early as 500 B.C. and flourished until about A.D. 600. They created a dazzling, wealthy society, prescribing their way of life on an area covering thousands of square miles and sending traders and emissaries over much of the continent. Wherever the Hopewell cultural influence reached, it became overwhelmingly dominant. Comparatively little is known of the Hopewell except that they practiced agriculture, studied astronomy, traveled long distances to trade, honored their dead, and believed in an afterlife. Beyond that, there is only speculation.

The Hopewell had an incredible fascination with death. Hopewell artists possessed the versatility and skill to shape art objects of

*Tall ironweed may grow 10 feet high in the meadows of Towner's Woods.*

immortal beauty to be buried with their dead. They created exquisite treasures that have endured through the ages. Hopewell life found its highest expression and expended its greatest efforts in meeting the mystery called death. With unknown words, extinct rituals, and artistic symbols, the Hopewell marked the pathway to eternity with elaborate craftsmanship and enigmatic earthworks.

Their earthen burial heaps were noted by the early white explorers and settlers of the Midwest, where nearly every major waterway was bordered by clusters of mounds. An estimated 10,000 existed in the Ohio Valley alone (although some were built by the earlier Adena). Most of these were burial mounds, but a few were the more puzzling effigy mounds and temple mounds. Archaeologists assigned the name Hopewell to this group of prehistoric people in the 1890s because one of the earliest and richest finds occurred on the Scioto Valley farm of Mordecai Hopewell, where more than 30 mounds were excavated in a 110-acre rectangular enclosure. We do not know what name these people gave themselves. Only a few of their small villages have been discovered, despite over a century and a half of archaeological research. The Hopewell keep their secrets well.

By A.D. 750 the Hopewell's distinctive way of life had dimmed and the burial sites were abandoned. The reason for the Hopewell demise is a mystery; conjecture suggests many factors, including social change, a breakdown in old patterns of trade, or warfare. The remaining Hopewell were likely absorbed into other tribes, but the answer probably will never be known. The Wyandot, Shawnee, and other Natives encountered by the first white men to reach the Midwest in the 1700s had no knowledge of who built the mounds or when. The disappearance of the Hopewell remains one of the great puzzles of American civilization.

The so-called historic tribes managed to hold on for only 54 years after the first white settlement in Ohio. The federal Indian Removal Act of 1842 forced the Wyandot from their last reservation at Upper Sandusky, marking the end of organized tribal life in Ohio.

The plows and bulldozers came to destroy many of the old mounds. And yet some mounds, like the one nestled in Towner's Woods, remain as haunting memorials of a lost civilization, famous in their own vicinities, but virtually unknown to Americans outside the old Hopewell kingdom. These are ancient places, places connected to times beyond our knowledge or understanding, places where the ancient ones walked and sang and read stories in the stars. At dusk, as the first stars come out, the waters of Lake Pippen give forth the solemn call of night herons or the gabble of geese settling in for the dark. Sometimes—if you stand alone while the vanishing light lengthens the shadows of the oak trunks and the wind off the lake brings the smell of night to the forest—it is possible to surrender to fantasy, to imagine timeless voices, to feel the weight of centuries, to sense the presence of the ghosts of departed greatness.

## Access

Drive north from Kent on OH 43. Turn right on Ravenna Road, about 2.5 miles north of downtown. Stay on Ravenna Road by forking right where Lake Rockwell Road goes left. Farther along, Ravenna Road doglegs sharply to the right to cross a railroad bridge, 2.2 miles from OH 43. Keep straight here to enter Towner's Woods on a short gravel road. The parking lot is marked by an old brick railroad building.

## Trail

Walk away from the building on a very broad trail through the woods, passing a gazebo on your right. Shortly reach a multitrail junction, with a drinking-water pump and a shelter. Turn left on a wide trail at about the 9 o'clock position and begin a slight ascent. The way leads past outhouses and through a small picnic area. Keep right at a fork and continue straight on the broad path where the narrow Lakeside Trail goes right.

Climb to the top of the Towner Mound, crowned with tall, straight red oaks, with some flowering dogwood in the sparse understory. This setting, with a 180-degree view of spirit-inhabited Lake Pippen, has awed visitors for millennia. At first glance, the conical mound resembles the rounded kames so prevalent in the park. But the mound reveals its artificial nature by its regularity and symmetry of shape. It evokes the image of a twilit people, fellow travelers whose tenure on earth is over. Within, archaeologists discovered human bones, weapons, tools, and jewelry, set aside before written time began. Fredric Ward Putnam, the "Father of American Archaeology," came from Harvard University's Peabody Museum to visit some of the Ohio mounds in 1883. He wrote: ". . . the mysterious work of an unknown people whose seemingly most sacred place we had invaded . . . There seemed to come to me a picture as of a distant time."

Descend to the right off the mound and continue to the right on a narrow path. The way veers left along a fence line and then climbs slightly to reach a T-intersection with the Lakeside Trail. Turn left. The double fence serves to prevent access to Lake Pippen, part of Akron's public water supply.

The Lakeside Trail follows the shoreline on the left as it climbs and descends kames surrounding the lake. It turns left where another path comes in from the right in the vicinity of outhouses. Farther along, a side trail joins from the right rear. The Eagle Trail comes in from the right rear and unites with the Lakeside Trail to cross a wood bridge and climb steps. At the top, reach a T-intersection with the broad cross-country ski course; turn left. Very shortly, follow the Eagle Trail as it turns left on a narrow path and descends steeply; a small trail shelter is on the right at this juncture.

The Eagle Trail angles away from the lake and eventually comes again to the wide cross-country ski trail at a T-intersection; turn left. Continue past the novice cross-counry ski trail to your right, then another side trail to your right, and walk through a scrubland of hawthorns, pin cherry, and multiflora rose. Enter a forest of second-growth saplings and pass the Ginseng Trail, which forks right at a large trail shelter. Your path continues along the left prong as it descends steeply. At the bottom, the large opening on your right (more easily seen during leafless seasons) is Barnacle Bog. The wetland is noted for its pure stand of leatherleaf, a low, northern shrub that is found in Ohio only in a few scattered locations on the glaciated Allegheny Plateau. Small, white, bell-like flowers bloom in clusters among the upper branches from March to July. Blanketing the ground beneath the leatherleaf is a lush carpet of sphagnum moss. A few wild calla, another northern plant rare in Ohio, are also found in Barnacle Bog.

Climb to the junction with Swann's Way, a side trail to your right, and continue straight as your path rises and falls with the hummocky topography. At the top of a hillock, come out of the woods where a side trail leads right, and continue straight downhill through a large meadow. The opening is pleasant at any time of the year, but it is spectacular in September when goldenrods are blooming. Some species reach a height of 6 feet.

Reach a big intersection at the top of a rise, with the way ahead broadening out into a wide, grassy expanse. Turn left here on a narrower trail, which soon curves right and descends. At the bottom are a picnic area and trails that lead off in various directions. Your way goes left into the woods on a wide trail at about the 9 o'clock position.

At a fork, keep left on a narrower trail that leads slightly uphill. Over the rise, descend steps and fork left again to continue down steps. The path leads along the park boundary bordering the railroad and soon reaches the parking lot.

# Mogadore Reservoir

## A car-shuttle hike
## on the Buckeye Trail

*Hiking distance: 7½ miles*
*Hiking time: 3½ hours*
*Maps: USGS Suffield; Buckeye Trail, Mogadore section*

This hike follows the blue-blazed Buckeye Trail along the north shore of Mogadore Reservoir from its swampy head, past North Dike, to near the concrete-and-earthen dam at the foot. Parts of the trail are overgrown in summer and at times difficult to follow, especially when the blazes are faded or absent. Poison ivy is common, and mosquitoes and decrflies are abundant in season. This walk is best done with two cars to avoid retracing your steps.

Mogadore Reservoir is a 1000-acre impoundment in southern Portage County owned and operated by the city of Akron. It was constructed in 1939 by damming the Little Cuyahoga River. The reservoir was designed to control flooding on the Little Cuyahoga, which had a history of washing out factories and homes in East Akron, and to serve as a source of water to run the city's rubber mills.

The 1930s and 1940s were holocaust years for riverine life in the United States. Spurred by the Federal Flood Control Act of 1938, a spate of dam-building turned free-running rivers into languid lakes. Most water-based animals are well adapted for living either in the flowing waters of rivers and streams or in the standing waters of lakes and ponds; relatively few thrive in both. When rivers are dammed, and flowing water is replaced by permanent reservoirs, many river species are placed at risk. Today there are 75,000 dams in the United States alone. The engineering frenzy resulted in a still-unfolding chain of ecological destruction. Now there are plans to unplug some of the nation's streams to save endangered fish and restore riparian wetlands by modifying the past manipulation of river systems. No

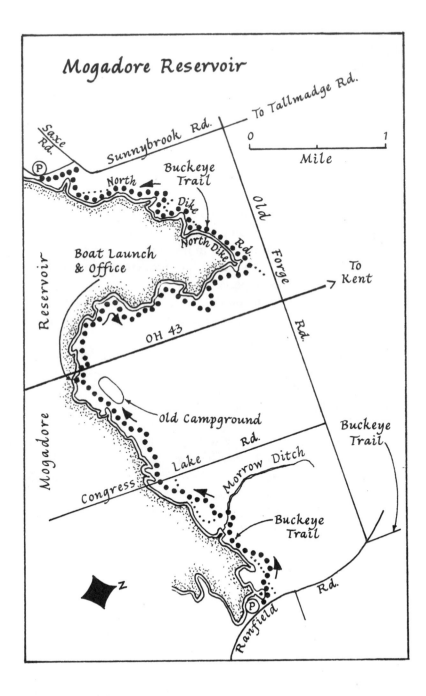

Mogadore Reservoir

such proposals have been put forth for the Little Cuyahoga.

The protected forests on the watershed lands are home to many species and Mogadore Reservoir itself is rich with animal life dependent on water. Anglers fish during every month of the year and birders know the reservoir as a prime spot to view a host of species, especially during spring and fall migrations. Duck hunters arrive during season to fill their daily bag limits. (No other hunting is allowed on city-owned land.) But the area has seen a shift in species composition from riverine fish such as sculpins, brook stickleback, and blacknose dace to lake fish such as bluegill, redear sunfish, and crappies; and from birds of rivers and bottomlands such as belted kingfisher and prothonotary warbler to water birds such as ring-billed gull, ducks, and grebes.

## Access

Drive south on OH 43 from Kent. Pass the intersections with the I-76 ramps and turn right at the next intersection (Tallmadge Road) in the hamlet of Brimfield. This junction is 3.8 miles from downtown Kent. Go 1.4 miles and turn left on Sunnybrook Road. Drive across Old Forge Road and fork left sharply to stay on Sunnybrook where Saxe Road goes right. You arrive in the vicinity of Mogadore Reservoir; leave the first car on the right in a gravel lot along Sunnybrook Road, 2.7 miles south of Tallmadge Road.

To reach your trailhead, go back north on Sunnybrook Road to Old Forge Road. Turn right, cross OH 43, and continue to a stop sign at Ranfield Road, 3.3 miles from where you turned onto Old Forge from Sunnybrook. Turn right on Ranfield and drive 0.9 mile to a small pullout on the right. The Buckeye Trail, which has followed Ranfield Road, turns right here to enter the watershed lands.

## Trail

Follow the blue paint blazes on a narrow trail as it winds through a mixed evergreen-deciduous forest. Cross a service road and, later, a wide, grassy swath. Continue straight in both places on the path.

The second time you encounter the service road, turn right and walk near the reservoir on your left. The road is used by patrol

*Kevin Birkley and Melissa Jolly near Mogadore Reservoir (Beverly J. Brown)*

vehicles and is closed to the public. The cinder road crosses Morrow Ditch on a wood bridge and climbs slightly. At the top of the rise, turn right off the road onto a grassy lane. Cross two more wide, mowed swaths. The trail narrows and becomes tangled in brush. Some bushwhacking may be necessary, but the way soon comes out once more onto the service road. Turn right.

As the road curves to the right, blazes indicate that the Buckeye Trail veers left into the woods, but the pathway is very overgrown and the dense undergrowth is virtually impenetrable. I suggest continuing on the service road, which shortly reaches Congress Lake Road. Turn left and walk about 1/10 mile toward the reservoir. Watch carefully for the continuing trailway on the right; it is a narrow path leading into the woods before you reach the guardrail along Congress Lake Road.

The foot trail is more obvious in this stretch as it trends eastward following the shoreline. Unmarked, informal paths begin to proliferate as you approach a former campground. Look carefully for the Buckeye Trail blazes and retrace your way if you discover you have made a wrong turn. The path comes out onto a road of broken asphalt and passes the old campground on your right.

The trail leads past a locked gate into a large, gravel parking area. Keep straight, passing the watershed office and a boat-launch ramp on the shore. Drinking water, rest rooms, and a telephone are here. Cross OH 43, get around a locked gate, and continue your hike on the service road.

The road intercepts or runs parallel to a gas pipeline along part of this stretch. The Buckeye Trail always stays on the service road, never on the mowed pipeline right-of-way. After walking about 2½ miles from OH 43, come upon another locked gate and turn left on North Dike Road, the former Saxe Road. This dirt road is open to vehicles during daylight hours from late March to late November, but traffic is usually light.

Pass North Dike on your left. The high dike keeps the waters of the reservoir from flooding a large scrub-shrub wetland on your right. Walking on the dike is prohibited.

The road climbs after the dike; the trail turns left at a small parking lot and enters the woods. The trailway is obscure through this area, but time and patience bring you back to North Dike Road. Turn left. The road climbs and curves left. After it straightens, the Buckeye Trail again veers left on a narrow path through the forest for a longer off-road section, but eventually returns to North Dike Road.

Pass a launch ramp and a large parking area. Farther on, encounter a small parking lot on the left as the road begins to climb. Turn left here to follow the trail along the water. The path loops around to come again onto what is now called Saxe Road near where it intersects with Sunnybrook Road. Turn left, walk to Sunnybrook, and turn left again. From here it is only about ¼ mile to the parking area and your planted car.

# Beaver Dam Trail

### A nature walk
### illustrating a dramatic comeback

*Hiking distance: 1 mile*
*Hiking time: 1 hour*
*Map: USGS Andover*

The French were the first white explorers to reach what became the Western Reserve. Their push into the interior of the continent was driven by an extraordinary market demand for fur, especially beaver pelts. The French were responding to a fashion craze that swept Europe after England's King Charles I declared in 1638: "Nothing but beaver stuff or beaver wool shall be used in the making of hats." (Coincidentally, it was Charles II, son of Charles I, who set up the Western Reserve when in 1662 he granted the Connecticut colony a charter to all lands in the New World between the 41st and 42nd parallels of north latitude.)

The French *voyageurs* paddled their way up the Great Lakes from Lower Canada (today's Quebec). The French are known to have been on Lake Erie during the middle of the 17th century, but another hundred years passed before they established a permanent place on the southern shore. In the 1740s François Saguin opened a trading post on the Cuyahoga River, and in the 1750s the French military built a line of fortifications along the lake, including Fort Presque Isle on the site of today's city of Erie and Fort Jonadat on Sandusky Bay.

France controlled the fur trade in the Great Lakes area for decades by arming the Native Americans with guns and traps. The French traders forged a relationship with Ohio tribes such as the Huron and the Ottawa. France used her Indian allies and her political, economic, and military power to successfully restrict the rival British to the American seaboard. England saw the New World as a place to expand her empire by clearing the land for settlement. The French and the Indians wished to keep the land in its natural state and

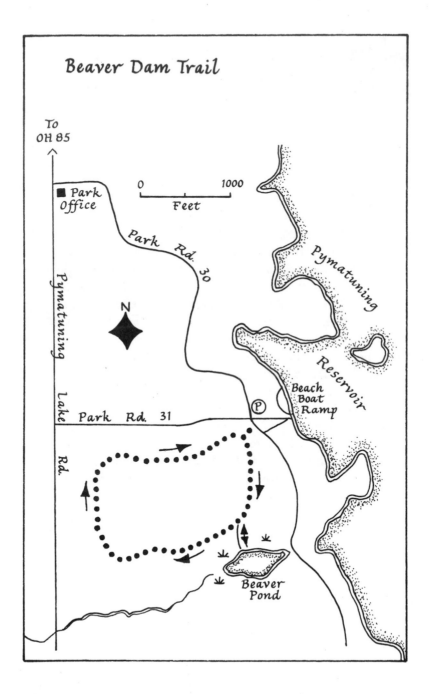

Beaver Dam Trail

continue to harvest its vast wealth in furs. Inevitably, skirmishes, battles, short wars, and ultimately a worldwide conflagration (called the French and Indian War in the American colonies) resulted.

In the end, the Native Americans, the French, and the British were forced to give up control of the Ohio lands. But the demand for beaver pelts continued. No one knows how many beaver skins were shipped from Ohio in our early history, but the numbers must have been immense. In 1785, John Heckewelder, a Moravian missionary among the Delaware Indians of Ohio, reported, "a Trader purchased 23 Horseload of peltry from the few Indians then hunting on [the Cuyahoga] River." Estimates of precolonial beaver numbers for the continent run anywhere from 60 to 400 million (compared with today's 6 to 12 million). By the late 1790s, beaver populations were in serious decline in the lower Great Lakes. The invention of the steel leghold trap in 1823 and the unceasing demand for beaver fur caused ruthless exploitation of the species. Another piece of Ohio wilderness disappeared in 1830 when the last beaver was trapped. At that time, the going price for a beaver pelt was $5.

Expanding cropland, accelerating deforestation, increasing drainage of wetlands, water pollution, and all of the attendant problems of rapid, uncontrolled growth made it seem unlikely that the beaver would ever return to Ohio. But a series of events in the 1930s in Ashtabula County and neighboring Pennsylvania provided the conditions that allowed beavers to reclaim part of their former range.

In 1931, Pennsylvania began to construct dams on the Shenango River to flood a vast swamp. The resulting Pymatuning Reservoir, mostly in Pennsylvania but partly in Ohio, was dedicated in 1934. The old Ohio Division of Conservation purchased land along the western shore in 1935 and began to manage the area for wildlife. In 1936, Ohio's first beaver colony in over a century was discovered in this wild-edged country.

Your short walk leads to the edge of a beaver pond in Pymatuning State Park, near the site of the recolonization in the mid-1930s. Beavers have returned to almost all areas of Ohio in such numbers that the state started a trapping season in 1960. Upwards of 5000 beavers are trapped every year in Ohio, usually making the Buckeye

*Pymatuning State Park's Beaver Dam Trail leads hikers through this forest.*

State second or third in the nation for beaver fur harvesting. Now as in colonial days most of America's pelts are shipped overseas; Europe currently consumes 70 percent of US fur exports. Today's beaver pelts bring an average of more than $11 each.

## Access

The Beaver Dam Trail is in Pymatuning State Park. From the square in Andover, drive east on OH 85 for 1.4 miles to Pymatuning Lake

Road. The intersection is just before OH 85 crosses the reservoir and is marked by a traffic signal. Turn right.

Drive another 1.4 miles to the main park entrance on your left. The park office is located here. Stop and pick up a trail pamphlet for today's walk.

Follow the main park route (Park Road 30) through the cabin area for 0.8 mile. Here there is a crossroad and the Beaver Dam Trail trailhead is on the far right corner. Turn left onto the drive that leads directly to a big, paved parking lot and leave your car. Panoramic views from the parking area reach over the water to the wooded Pennsylvania shore, also protected as a state park. Walk across Park Road 30 to reach the trail entrance.

## Trail

In the early days of America's colonization, no one appreciated a good woods more than the French fur traders. That is exactly what you will find along the Beaver Dam Trail. Here, where the upland beech–sugar maple forest mingles with the lowland elm–red maple forest, beaver and other wildlife are abundant.

Your walk begins in a beautiful mature forest of sugar maple and American beech. More than 50 percent of Ashtabula County is wooded, the most of any county in the Western Reserve. Take the left fork and follow the numbered stations.

Eastern chipmunks whistle a warning of your approach before they duck out of sight behind a log or into a burrow. May-apple, wild geranium, and other woodland flowers carpet the ground in spring. Touch-me-not can be found in low, wet places in the forest.

The land is gently rolling. After station 5, turn left on a spur that leads to the edge of a beaver pond. Soon evidences of beaver activity are noticed—a downed tree, gnawed branches. The spur ends at the water. Catching sight of a beaver in the pond or even on the shore requires patience, quietness, and luck. Your chances are increased if you are hiking in early morning or near dusk, since beavers are nocturnal.

Retrace your steps to the main path. There, turn left to continue on the nature trail. Skirt a wetland near station 7. Around station 8 is a small clearing where the autumn flowers of open fields put on a colorful display. Goldenrods and at least three species of aster can be found. The forest beyond the clearing is much younger. The trees are reclaiming an old field that was cultivated in the early 1900s. Red maples are the predominant tree here, although a few black cherries grow on the drier portions. Chipmunks are not as common here as in the old woods.

Cross a small wetland on a short boardwalk beyond station 13 and pass through a little grove of magnificent pin oak. Your path reenters the mature forest and comes out at the trailhead.

# Warren

## A stroll through the
## Western Reserve's early metropolis

*Hiking distance: 2¾ miles*
*Hiking time: 2 hours*
*Maps: USGS Champion and Warren*

Warren was established in 1799 by Ephraim Quinby, who named the settlement in honor of Moses Warren, one of the surveyors in Moses Cleaveland's expedition for the Connecticut Land Company. A year later, the Reverend Joseph Badger, a minister sent out by the Missionary Society of Connecticut, found 11 families residing in Warren, more than anyplace else in the Reserve. In 1800, the governor of the Northwest Territory, Arthur St. Clair, named Warren "capital of the County of Trumbull," which at that time included the entire Western Reserve. Warren's location, on the Mahoning River with relatively easy access to Pittsburgh and the Ohio River, assured its growth and early success.

By 1812 Warren boasted the Western Reserve's first bank—the Western Reserve Bank—and its first newspaper—*The Trump of Fame.* An early settler, Ohio Supreme Court judge Rufus P. Spalding, wrote in 1823: "The village of Warren . . . was considered as altogether ahead of Cleveland in importance. The population was estimated at four hundred souls."

Things had changed by 1830, after Cleveland became the lake port for the Ohio & Erie Canal. Warren continued to grow, but at a slower pace. It was incorporated as a city in 1869, when it was home to 4500 people. The mills and factories of Warren were mostly small family businesses typical of a county seat river town with a surrounding agricultural community. By 1910 the population had reached 11,000, while underground a peaceful revolution was simmering in the city. Young, aggressive businessmen had organized a Board of Trade in 1905. A well-publicized, high-pressure campaign was

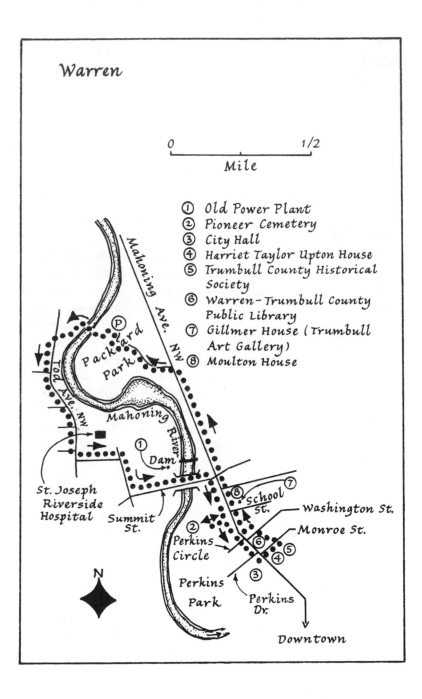

Warren

0             1/2
Mile

① Old Power Plant
② Pioneer Cemetery
③ City Hall
④ Harriet Taylor Upton House
⑤ Trumbull County Historical Society
⑥ Warren–Trumbull County Public Library
⑦ Gillmer House (Trumbull Art Gallery)
⑧ Moulton House

mounted to boost the city and persuade industry to move to Warren. The board bought up land on the river flats and offered free sites to companies to build their plants. In 1912, Trumbull Steel Company opened as Warren's first big steel firm when they agreed to locate six mills on the donated land. The *Warren Tribune* reported, "Warren's largest industry is well on its way to what is predicted a huge success."

The 1920 census shows Warren's population had jumped 130 percent to 27,050. Immigrants (mostly from Italy, Slovenia, Croatia, and Serbia) flocked to the city's factories. A housing boom resulted in the construction of 3000 new homes on the Mahoning Flats and around the steel mills on the south side of town. The Mahoning Valley became the second leading steel-producing region in the United States. After World War II, the Mahoning mills entered a long and steady decline. Most of the factories closed in the late 1970s and early 1980s. Nearly 25,000 valley steelworkers lost their jobs in four years.

Your circuit walk explores the old streets north of Courthouse Square, where Warren's early settlers planted their Yankee values, and crosses the Mahoning to skirt a small section of industrial Warren, now rusting and overgrown. The city is in the process of discovering all facets of its long past as it prepares for its Bicentennial in 1999. As historian Harlan Hatcher points out, Warren "still remembers that it was the capital of the Western Reserve before Ohio became a state . . . and that it was a populous center of life when Cleveland was still a struggling and sickly village on the sand-choked Cuyahoga." Look for the old sandstone block sidewalks along the way.

## Access

From Courthouse Square in downtown Warren, drive north on Mahoning Avenue NW for 1.1 miles to Packard Park on your left. Follow the drive as it winds through the park for 0.3 mile to the vicinity of McGregor Field. Park on the bluff above the athletic field or in the lower lot between the field and the Mahoning River.

## Trail

Lying on the river's left bank, 43-acre Packard Park was donated to the city in 1911 by Warren native William D. Packard. William and his brother, James, established the Packard Electric Company in Warren in 1899 for the manufacture of lightbulbs, transformers, lamp sockets, and other such products. The Packard brothers also were interested in another new invention, the horseless carriage. Warren did not have the capital to support such a large venture as automobile manufacturing, so James gained financial backing in Cleveland, where he formed the Ohio Automobile Company and began making automobiles in 1899. In 1903 Packard reorganized his business and moved to Detroit as the Packard Motor Car Company. Packard Electric eventually was absorbed by General Motors, which still operates in Warren today.

Cross the Mahoning River on the footbridge. The river here resembles the idyllic 19th-century stream familiar to composer Stephen Foster, whose sister lived in Warren. His visits and walks along the Mahoning reportedly inspired a handful of musical compositions. Unseen to the casual observer, however, today's river bears the burden of almost seven decades of industrial abuse. The stretch below you, extending from just upriver to the Pennsylvania border 25 miles downstream, was placed on a swimming, wading, and fish consumption advisory by the Ohio Department of Health in 1988. The *Christian Science Monitor* had labeled the Mahoning "America's hottest and dirtiest river" in 1946. The newspaper reported that the Mahoning was "probably the country's most thoroughly industrialized stream. Lined with giant steel mills, railroads, fabricating plants, and power-generating plants, waters in the stream . . . are used over and over again, 10 to 20 times."

The river carries a deadly brew of pesticides, phthalate esters, and polychlorinated biphenyls, but its chief affliction is probably the presence of polynuclear aromatic hydrocarbons (PAH) in the bottom sediment. The PAH group of compounds is hazardous to humans and wildlife, and some of them are listed as carcinogenic. Their presence in the Mahoning is the result of years of discharging the by-products of coking operations into the river.

Paradoxically, the stream now meets the water quality standards set by the Ohio Environmental Protection Agency. Thus, the Mahoning is a river with fairly good water flowing over highly contaminated sediment. The river has made a remarkable recovery in the 20 years since the collapse of the local steel industry. Exhortations to improve the Mahoning go back at least as far as 1924, but recent efforts cite the recreational and environmental benefits of a healthy river, with a goal to achieve significant cleanup for the city's bicentennial celebration.

The paved trail on the right bank winds through a riparian forest and climbs out of the floodplain to reach Tod Avenue NW. Cross the street and turn left. The avenue is named for David Tod, a prominent early resident of Warren who served as postmaster (1832–1838) and mayor (1838). He continued his public service as US ambassador to Brazil and was elected governor of Ohio during the Civil War era.

Walk past St. Joseph Riverside Hospital on your left and stay on Tod Avenue as it curves left and then right around the hospital. Cross a railroad and reach Summit Street at a traffic signal. Turn left on Summit and descend to cross the Mahoning again on a highway bridge built in 1931. The large, dilapidated, and abandoned brick structure on your left is an old electric power plant. Warren's first generating plant was built on this site in 1890 and expanded over the years. Originally run by the city, the plant was taken over by Ohio Edison, which continued its operation until 1977, when Warren's economy begin to crumble. The Summit Street crossing is near the site of the first dam on the river, built in 1802. The present dam at the power plant is one of ten low-head dams on the Mahoning from Warren downstream to Lowellville. Riverfront industries originally built these small dams to create pools of water for industrial intake. The dams have outlived their usefulness and now only obstruct the passage of fish and canoes. Proposals have been put forth to remove the dams as part of the Mahoning's restoration.

Climb to Mahoning Avenue NW and turn right. Mahoning is old Warren's elegant street. First laid out in 1819, it became the center of the city's wealth and prestige. This is the street Hatcher described in his 1949 history of the Western Reserve: "In the north section of the town some of the older families, holding onto the Connecticut heritage, preserved their ancestral homes." Townsfolk call it Millionaires' Row, but millionaire status was perhaps awarded

*The old electric power plant on the Mahoning River in Warren*

more loosely by gossip than by actual accumulated riches. Warren's Millionaires' Row rivaled similar streets elsewhere in the Reserve in Cleveland, Youngstown, and Norwalk. The Mahoning Avenue Historic District was listed on the National Register of Historic Places in 1971. It remains today remarkably intact and well preserved as a monument to the moneyed and landed families who built their mansions on the high ground overlooking the Mahoning River.

Walk a short distance to the Trumbull County Chapter of the American Red Cross. Behind the chapter house is the Pioneer Cemetery, a quiet, shady tract on a bluff overlooking the river. The graveyard, one of the oldest in the Western Reserve, was donated by

Henry Lane Jr. in 1804. A small memorial on the left after you enter the grounds lists the 12 Revolutionary War veterans who settled in Warren and are buried here. Interments ceased in 1848. Continue south along the avenue, cross Perkins Circle and Perkins Drive, and reach the city hall at 391 Mahoning. Known as the Perkins House, the Victorian-Italianate building was built in 1871 by Henry B. Perkins Sr., president of First National Bank (a successor to the original Western Reserve Bank). The city moved into the house in 1931. Visitors are welcome during normal operating hours; brochures are available and impromptu tours may take place. Behind city hall is 35-acre Perkins Park.

Cross the street to an earlier Henry B. Perkins Sr. home standing at the corner of Mahoning Avenue and Monroe Street. Perkins built this house in the Greek Revival style in the late 1830s and lived here after his marriage in 1855 until the new house across the street was constructed. Ezra B. Taylor purchased the house from Henry in 1871. Ezra was a judge, a US representative, and the father of Harriet Taylor. While living in Washington, Harriet became an activist for women's rights. There, she also met George Upton, a lawyer; the couple married in Warren in 1884. Ezra deeded the home at 380 Mahoning Avenue to his daughter "for love and affection and as an advancement." In Warren, Harriet continued her crusade while George practiced patent law for many of the city's leading businessmen, including the Packard brothers. Harriet served as treasurer for the National American Woman Suffrage Association around the turn of the century, and Warren became a center for the effort to gain the vote for women. The association's headquarters was in Harriet's house for a short time and then later moved to a wing of the courthouse. She played a leading role in the successful ratification of the 19th Amendment to the Constitution in 1920. Harriet also wrote *History of the Western Reserve,* one of the earliest books focusing on the Reserve, in 1910. The house is named the Harriet Taylor Upton House in her honor and is operated by the Upton Association. Tours of the house and the Upton Memorial Gardens in the back yard can be arranged in advance by calling the Upton Association at 216-395-1131; donations are accepted. The house is a National Historic Landmark and is listed on the National Register of Historic Places.

Walk down Monroe Street to number 303, the Edwards home. John Stark Edwards built this house in 1807, and it is today the oldest frame structure in Trumbull County, perhaps in the Western Reserve. In 1813, newspaperman Thomas Webb (editor of *The Trump of Fame*) bought the house. The structure was originally on South Street but was moved to its present location in 1986. The home is listed on the National Register of Historic Places and is operated as a museum by the Trumbull County Historical Society. The building is open Sunday and Wednesday 2–4 and at other times by appointment; call 216-394-4653 beforehand. Admission is charged. For sale at the museum is *An Historic Walk along Mahoning Avenue,* a small guidebook offering more detail about the architecture and history of the neighborhood.

Cross Monroe Street and walk through the parking lot behind the Warren–Trumbull County Public Library. The library houses the Sutliff Museum on the second floor. The museum features the 19th-century belongings and furnishings of the Levi Sutliff family. The museum is open Tuesday through Saturday 2:30–4:30, but is closed Saturdays in the summer; free. Reach Washington Street and turn left to come again onto Mahoning Avenue. Turn right on Mahoning and pass a succession of private houses built between the 1850s and 1900.

Cross School Street and reach the Trumbull Art Gallery at 720 Mahoning Avenue. Built in 1854 by Thomas Jefferson McLain, the building is usually called the Gillmer House after industrialist Elmer Wood Gillmer. The Gillmer family lived here from 1894 to 1969. The Trumbull Art Gallery is free and is open Sunday 1–4 and Tuesday through Friday noon–4. The gallery specializes in exhibitions featuring Ohio artists and mounts about eight shows per year. A visit to the gallery also includes a tour of the house, which is listed on the National Register of Historic Places.

At 736 Mahoning is the Moulton House, built around 1906 by Edwin Moulton, superintendent of Warren City Schools. It is currently the Twin Maples Bed & Breakfast. Continue north on Mahoning Avenue to return to Packard Park.

# Mosquito Lake State Park

## Through fields and forests beside a big reservoir

*Hiking distance: 1½ miles*
*Hiking time: 1 hour*
*Map: USGS Cortland*

Most of the rivers and creeks of the Western Reserve are short and flow north off the plateau into Lake Erie. A narrow belt along the southern border of the central portion of the Reserve is in the Ohio River basin. In the eastern part of the Western Reserve, the Ohio Valley bulges far to the north, reaching as close as 20 miles from the Lake Erie shore. This is the region of big, south-flowing rivers like the Mahoning and the Shenango. The uplands stretching across the Continental Divide are exceptionally level and poorly drained. They are the old glacial flats left behind after the land was scoured by the last great continental ice sheet. In places the distance between north- and south-flowing creeks is short, so that rain falling on the swamp flats may make its way into either the Great Lakes or the Ohio River.

Mosquito Creek is a good example of the intimacy of the two watersheds. The creek flows south into the Mahoning River along the east side of an oblong basin that stretches north from Warren toward the Erie shore. On the west side of this valley curves the Grand River, flowing north to the lake. When Mosquito Creek was dammed in the 1940s, the US Army Corps of Engineers designed an uncontrolled "natural" spillway in the northwest reach of the reservoir. The normal pool elevation is about 901 feet above sea level, but if floods raise the water level to 904 feet, the southerly outflow of the reservoir is reversed and water flows north into the Grand River valley.

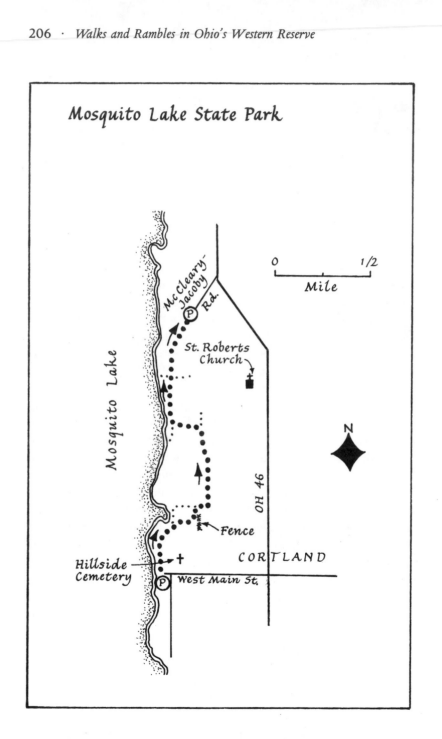

Mosquito Lake State Park

Mosquito Lake boasts an impressive list of statistics. About 10 miles long and over 1 mile wide at its broadest point, it covers 7850 acres and has 44 miles of shoreline. It is the largest inland lake in the Western Reserve and the second largest in Ohio. The dam across Mosquito Creek is 47 feet high, 430 feet thick at its base, and 5650 feet long.

Mosquito Lake State Park is second in size among state parks in the Western Reserve (only West Branch is larger). It offers extensive water recreation opportunities, but trail choices for walkers are limited. The park has two short hiking paths, one in the campground (1¼ miles) and another in the picnic area (¼ mile). Trails for equestrians and snowmobilers are extensive, but these are poorly maintained for foot travelers. The rough trail described here follows the snowmobile route on the east side of the reservoir. The trailway is shown inaccurately on the park map; follow the directions below.

There is disagreement about the correct name for the park and reservoir. Mosquito Lake State Park is the most commonly accepted name, but the big sign at the main entrance reads Mosquito State Park. Other signs and some park literature refer to Mosquito Creek State Park. The USGS map labels it Mosquito Creek Lake State Park. The impoundment is called Mosquito Lake or Mosquito Creek Reservoir by the state and Mosquito Creek Lake by the US Army Corps of Engineers. Adding to the mix is the state-owned Mosquito Creek Wildlife Area at the north end of the reservoir. "Mosquito" is the one common word among all of these titles, and it is apt. About 60 species of mosquitoes occur in the Western Reserve, and there are times when you may feel that all of them are found on this trail. Mosquitoes and other biting flies are voracious in the low woods and wet meadows; bring repellent for your hike here in the warmer months. The pathway is overgrown in places in summer and is very wet in the rainy seasons. All-terrain vehicles have created deep, muddy, water-filled ruts on many of the trails. Waterproof hiking boots are recommended. Hunting is allowed in this section of the park, so exercise caution during big-game season. This hike is best done with two cars to avoid retracing your route, but the distance is relatively short, so a return along the same path is easy.

## Access

To drop off the first car, take OH 46 north from Cortland. Turn left on McCleary-Jacoby Road (Trumbull County Road 201), a small lane that angles to the left rear where OH 46 curves right. No sign is posted at this intersection. The turn is 1.6 miles north of the intersection of OH 46 and West Main Street in Cortland and 0.5 mile north of St. Roberts Catholic Church, a prominent landmark on your left as you drive north on OH 46. Drive a short distance to the end of McCleary-Jacoby Road where a gate marks the state park boundary. Park your car away from the houses on the lane but do not block access to the gate.

To reach the southern trailhead, return to Cortland and turn right on West Main Street. Drive 0.5 mile to the foot of West Main and leave your car in the large state park lot.

## Trail

Walk north on the trail by the water. Hillside Cemetery is upslope on your right. Follow the graveyard fence to near the end and then angle slightly left into a thicket to continue on the path. The way passes through a marshy meadow and crosses two small runs. A broad side trail goes to the right, but it is usually so overgrown in the summer that it may not be readily apparent. Continue straight.

After about ¼ mile you will reach a wide, mowed, grassy swath (a sewer right-of-way). The trail ahead is waterlogged and impassable most of the time, so turn right and walk up the sewer line. Before you reach a chain-link fence, turn left on a track through an old field. Walk through the shrubby field, passing over a culverted drainageway, and soon reach a T-intersection. Turn right and walk slightly uphill. You may notice a rusty sign that says "Stay on Trail" nailed to a tree along this stretch. The track curves left and passes across a low, sandy hillock capped with a small grove of quaking aspen. Descend gradually and reenter the old field environment before reaching a dense forest.

The woods have a few beech, hickories, and black cherry growing on the higher, drier knolls, but mostly you walk through a lowland forest of pin oak, red maple, silver maple, green ash, and

*Mosquito Lake is the largest reservoir in the Western Reserve.*

elms. Note the faint, irregular yellow paint blazes on some of the trees, an indicator that you are on the right path.

Follow the more obvious trail left where a fainter, less-used trail goes straight and downhill. You soon also descend to cross a small run. Climb the low ridge on the other side, then walk down a gentle incline toward the reservoir and a little beach. Near the water's edge you will find a straight trail going both left and right. Turn right (north) and walk along an abandoned road, the former McCleary-Jacoby Road. The old roadbed is built above the wetlands, so the way before you is much drier than what you have traversed thus far. Good views of the reservoir can be had through the trees before the trail and the shore recede from each other.

Low sandstone abutments mark the course of a drainageway under the former road. Shortly beyond, come to a cross trail. The broad way to your right winds to St. Roberts Church on OH 46. A short walk to your left leads you through a small meadow to a narrow sandy beach. Continue straight on the old road and you soon reach the place where you parked your second car.

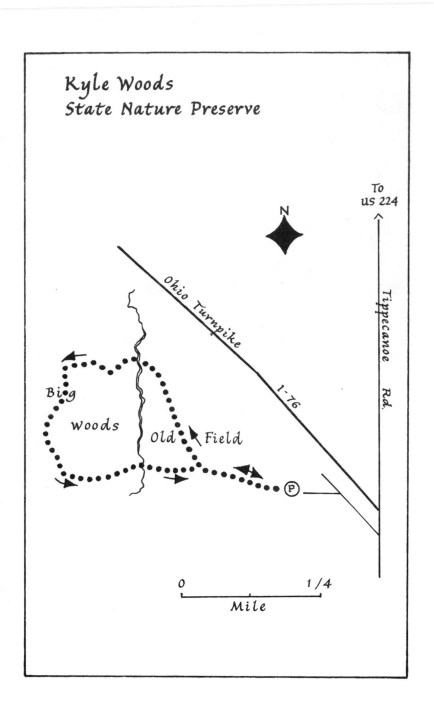

Kyle Woods
State Nature Preserve

# Kyle Woods
# State Nature Preserve

## One of the Western Reserve's
## last undisturbed forests

*Hiking distance: 1 mile*
*Hiking time: ½ hour*
*Maps: USGS Youngstown; state nature preserve map*

The short trail at Kyle Woods State Nature Preserve is called the Sugarbush Trail because it passes through a grove of sugar maples, or sugarbush, where maple sap was collected to make maple syrup. The old forest at the preserve has its share of sugar maple and American beech trees, the forest type so common in much of the Western Reserve. Ohio's beech-maple belt extends from Pennsylvania as far west as Mansfield. Kyle Woods, near the southern border of the Western Reserve, is also near an ill-defined boundary where the beech and maple trees of Northeast Ohio, nourished by cloudy days, cool summer temperatures, and heavy winter snow cover, begin to yield to the mixed forests of the poorer, unglaciated soils of the southeast, where the climate is sunnier, warmer, and drier. The little preserve, due to its location near this borderland of plant habitats, contains a remarkable diversity of hardwoods for its size. Over 25 species of broadleaf trees have been recorded from Kyle Woods, including (in addition to sugar maple and American beech) black cherry, white ash, red oak, white oak, tulip tree, shagbark hickory, cucumber magnolia, sour gum, hornbeam, and sassafras. Most botanists refer to this blend of hardwoods as a mixed mesophytic forest.

Arthur Kyle purchased the farm with the "Big Woods" in 1903. The preserve brochure describes Kyle as a "farmer who loved his woods." He cultivated the fields and ran a maple syrup operation in the sugarbush for over half a century. Other than the late-winter

*A water-filled depression created by a windfallen tree (Beverly J. Brown)*

sugaring, the woods remained largely undisturbed. Giant trees and luxuriant spring wildflowers can be seen from your trail, a legacy from a family who loved the land on which they lived—not loving it in an abstract sense, but knowing it, growing crops on it, making syrup from maple trees on it, gathering berries on it, hunting on it, strolling through it.

Arthur Kyle would likely echo the words of essayist Katie Laur: "I love trees. I like their rough, gnarly bark . . . the crooked way that some of them have grown just to survive. I saw their great branches reaching toward the sun for nourishment, saw them hold their ground in storms and drought." The surviving forests still hold treasures, shouldering the intricate life patterns of their plant and animal communities and the ecological balances that sustain them.

## Access

Kyle Woods State Nature Preserve is in Canfield Township, Mahoning County. From the Canfield Green, drive east on US 224 for 2.4 miles to Tippecanoe Road in the hamlet of Starr's Corners. Turn right. (OH 625 goes left at this intersection.) Follow Tippecanoe Road south for

0.6 mile. Pass under the twin spans of the Ohio Turnpike (I-76) and immediately turn right onto a road leading to a turnpike garage. No sign marks this intersection. Go just 0.1 mile and turn left into the preserve. The narrow gravel entrance road leads steeply uphill to a small parking lot.

## Trail

The path leads through a fence opening and along a mowed swath across a field slowly reverting to forest. Saplings of white ash, tulip tree, and cherry are interspersed among thickets of silky dogwood. The herbaceous layer is rich, with grasses, goldenrods, milkweeds, asters, and Indian hemp forming a colorful ground cover. Where the trail divides, keep right and meander through more of the old field before curving left to enter the Big Woods, one of the best examples of a mature mixed hardwood forest remaining in Ohio.

The verdant forest stands on the highest land in the preserve. Scattered throughout the woods are the sugar maple trees that served such an important function on the Kyle family farm. Sugaring ceased in the 1950s, partly because the Ohio Turnpike split the property and separated the sugarbush from the farm buildings.

The narrow path is easy to follow as it weaves through the lush woods and emerges again into the field. Short boardwalks lift the trail above some of the quaggy areas. Return to the entrance spur and retrace your way to the parking lot.

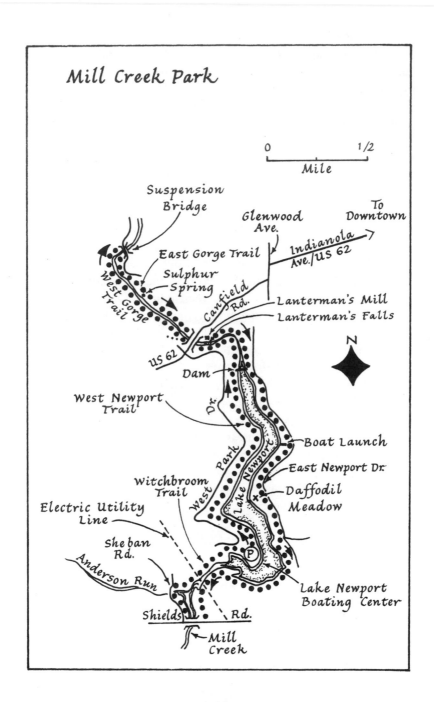

# Mill Creek Park

0           1/2

Mile

Suspension Bridge

Glenwood Ave.

To Downtown

East Gorge Trail

Indianola Ave./US 62

Sulphur Spring

West Gorge Trail

Canfield Rd.

Lanterman's Mill

Lanterman's Falls

US 62

N

Dam

West Newport Trail

Dr.

Boat Launch

West Park Dr.

East Newport Dr.

Lake Newport

Daffodil Meadow

Witchbroom Trail

Electric Utility Line

Sheban Rd.

P

Anderson Run

Lake Newport Boating Center

Shields     Rd.

Mill Creek

# Mill Creek Park

### "One of the most beautiful spots in the Western Reserve"

*Hiking distance: 6¾ miles*
*Hiking time: 3 hours*
*Maps: USGS Youngstown; park map*

Mill Creek Park was established in Youngstown in 1891, making it one of the oldest parks in the Western Reserve. Its unlikely birth came in the midst of a great economic depression in the city. A protracted labor dispute between steelworkers and the Mahoning Valley steel companies had throttled Youngstown for months. The strike had spread into Ohio from Pennsylvania, bringing with it a host of idle, restless laborers with a penchant for violence and bloodshed. The fires of the valley's blast furnaces were extinguished and the city's residents faced an uncertain future of misery and starvation. Soup kitchens were set up and charities were organized to keep the working families going.

In this troubled time, lawyer, civic leader, and outdoorsman Volney Rogers proposed the acquisition of a large park in the Mill Creek Valley. Volney single-handedly fashioned the park, lobbying for legislation and persuading the financially strapped city to issue bonds to purchase Mill Creek. He personally subscribed to $25,000 worth of park bonds when they were issued, insisting that his bonds be the last to be redeemed. Hundreds of steel men were put to work in the new park, building roads and trails and cutting picnic areas out of the forest. Each man was given three days of work each week for $1 a day. Volney moved to the park, where he built cabins and collapsible houses at several sites so he could keep an eye on the progress. He was described as a "great walker" and took daily morning and evening walks along Mill Creek and its tributaries.

Volney's imprint on the park as it is today cannot be overstated. For 29 years, he prepared every deed and contract, brought or defended every lawsuit, learned surveying so he could prepare topographical maps, and learned landscape architecture so he could plan park improvements, all without pay. Volney was concerned about every living thing in the park, especially birds. He personally planted winter wheat to sustain birds through the cold months, built brush shelters for songbirds, and instituted an interest and appreciation for birds in local schools to discourage neighborhood boys from killing them.

Volney's legacy is a grand park that is famed for rich green woods, the cool surge of Mill Creek, and 15 miles of hiking trails. Underfoot are the changing textures of hemlock needles, water-polished rock, boardwalk, and streambeds. Historian Harlan Hatcher described the Mill Creek Valley as "one of the most beautiful spots in the Western Reserve." John C. Melnick, author of a 446-page book about the park, wrote, "Mill Creek Park is the most priceless possession of the people of Youngstown and Mahoning County." Perhaps the most vivid portrayal is Volney Rogers' description of walking in the park: "I found the scenery delightful, the trees, rocks, cliffs, waterfalls, mosses, shrubs, wildflowers and birds enchanting, the air invigorating, the cool springs clear and healthful and I would return from these walks refreshed, happy in the remembrance of something new which I had learned from the book of nature." May you also return from your walk in Mill Creek Park "refreshed" and "happy in the remembrance."

## Access

From downtown Youngstown, drive south on Market Street (US 62) and cross the Mahoning River on the Vietnam Veterans Memorial Bridge. Stay on US 62 as it turns right on Indianola Avenue, left on Glenwood Avenue, and right on Canfield Road. Cross Mill Creek and turn left on West Park Drive into Mill Creek Park; this intersection is 3.6 miles from downtown. West Park Drive winds south through the park. After 1.6 miles, turn left into the Lake Newport Boating Center; no sign marks the entrance.

## Trail

From the parking area, head north across the open field/picnic area. Find a path that enters the woods between a small parking lot and the

*Ninety-foot high Lanterman's Mill and twenty-three-foot high Lanterman's Falls*

lake. Your way is the narrow, shady West Newport Trail that runs along the edge of Lake Newport, an old impoundment on Mill Creek that is largely silted in. A few areas of open water remain, but mostly the reservoir resembles a marsh, with extensive stands of emergent aquatic vegetation. Ducks and herons are partial to the wetlands created by the aging lake. West Park Drive parallels your trail upslope to the left.

Walk through a small picnic area, with tables and rest rooms, and reenter the woods. The lake opens up more as you approach the dam. At 60 acres, Lake Newport is the largest of the park's three reservoirs. Keep right where the trail forks and descend to the foot of the dam, a 1928 structure built of huge sandstone blocks. The dam is 18 feet high and 140 feet wide. Your path, the West Gorge Trail, continues along the creek as it skitters through a narrow ravine. Eastern hemlocks cling to the steep slopes and canopy the trail, forming a deep, dense shade. The sandstone cliffs are largely covered with ferns, mosses, liverworts, and lichens.

Where the trail forks, go left, curving uphill on steps. Reach a narrow, paved service road and continue uphill by walking straight. The road descends to your right to cross Mill Creek on a covered bridge. Near the gate at the top of the ridge, rejoin your woods trail, which descends and goes under Canfield Road. Beyond the highway bridge, the trail forks again; keep right. The path passes an overhanging rock shelter and other sandstone outcrops as it descends again to near the water. Numerous seeps feed beds of skunk cabbage on small level areas along the creek.

The West Gorge Trail ends at the Suspension Bridge over Mill Creek. The span was built in 1895 as a true suspension bridge, but a center pier was added for support in 1973. Cross the bridge and follow the road south for a short distance. As the road curves slightly to the left and begins an ascent, keep straight and level on the East Gorge Trail as it follows the creek upstream.

Pass Sulphur Spring, now dry. The spring was opened in 1884 during test drilling in search of coal. Around the turn of the century, a few local doctors prescribed the spring's mineral water for some of their patients with rheumatism.

As the gorge narrows, wooden steps lead up to a long boardwalk suspended from the cliff face. The boardwalk descends and ascends to follow the contour of the rock, then comes out at the Canfield Road bridge. Walk under the bridge and reach Lanterman's Mill and Lanterman's Falls.

The massive gristmill was built in 1845–1846 by German Lanterman and Samuel Kimberly. It was the third mill to be constructed at the 23-foot-high falls. The earliest mill, dating from 1799, was one of the first to be built in the Western Reserve. The mill's walls are nearly 10 feet thick at creek level and the building rises 90 feet from the water to the roof comb. Lanterman's Mill closed in 1888, unable to compete economically with the more efficient roller mills used for grinding grain. The park acquired the building in 1892. The US Department of the Interior placed the structure on the National Register of Historic Places in 1976. By that time, the mill was severely dilapidated. In the 1980s, Mill Creek Metropolitan Park District began a painstaking restoration of the old mill. The work took over three years and $600,000. Lanterman's Mill is once again running and offers stone-ground cornmeal, buckwheat, and whole wheat flour for sale in the gift shop. Rest rooms and drinking water are here. The mill is open May through October (closed Monday). Part of the restorative effort included the 1988 construction of the covered bridge just upstream of the falls. It replaces a 19th-century covered bridge that stood on the same site.

Continue upstream past the mill on a broad gravel path. Your trail climbs to near a road, levels, then descends to the creek. Reach the foot of the Lake Newport dam and climb steps to the top. Your path joins East Newport Drive, a park road where automotive traffic is restricted to one lane northbound.

Pass the East Newport Boat Launch and the Daffodil Meadow. Where a road comes in from the left, turn right on a broad, mowed swath, leaving East Newport Drive. The way leads close to the water, then turns left on a narrow trail through the forest. The swampy, upper reaches of Lake Newport are close by on your right.

Go under an electric utility line and reach Shields Road. Turn right to cross Mill Creek, then turn right on Sheban Drive and right again immediately onto the Witchbroom Trail. Your way shortly returns to Sheban Drive to cross Anderson Run, then reenters the forest.

Keep right, close to the creek, where trails fork left to climb steps. The path remains in the forest except for a brushy area under the power line. The trail climbs steps to reach the parking lot at the Lake Newport boathouse.

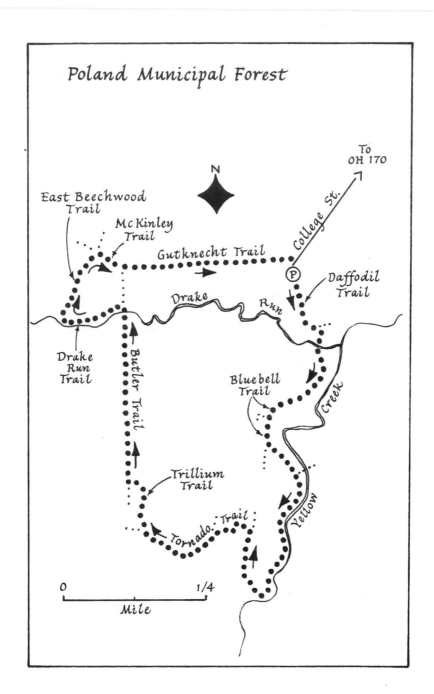

Poland Municipal Forest

# Poland
# Municipal Forest

Magnificent plant life,
including unmatched trees
and luxuriant wildflowers

*Hiking distance: 1¾ miles*
*Hiking time: 1 hour*
*Maps: USGS Campbell and Youngstown; municipal forest map*

I n the 1840s, historian Henry Howe made extended journeys over Ohio, talking with people, sketching scenes, and recording the passing era. The result of his field work was the unique and priceless *Historical Collections of Ohio,* in which he wrote about Poland: ". . . it is one of neatest villages in the state. The dwellings are usually painted white, and have an air of comfort . . . the surrounding country . . . is fertile."

Howe's words ring true today, 150 years later. The citizens of Poland have retained the New England air in the village and have set aside part of their fertile surroundings as a municipal forest, the first in Ohio and one of the few of its kind in the state or country. The 250-acre forest, established in 1938, preserves outstanding tracts of bottomland forest along Yellow Creek and Drake Run, as well as fine examples of upland beech–sugar maple forest and lowland elm red maple forest. The herbaceous understory is especially rich, beginning with the first woodland flowers of early spring and continuing with the less plentiful but still colorful forest flowers of mid- to late summer. Depending on the time of your visit, you can find skunk cabbage, Virginia bluebell, trilliums, spring beauty, hepatica, wild geranium, toothworts, May-apple, false Solomon's seal, blue cohosh, mints, cardinal flower, touch-me-not (both spotted and pale), asters, and many others.

An extensive trail network courses through the forest. The circuit hike described here is just one of many possibilities. Forest maps are available from the Municipal Building, 308 Main St., Poland, OH 44514 (216-757-2112). The map shows many trails that no longer exist. The Bluebell Trail is open to vehicular traffic when the Virginia bluebells are in bloom. The Village Hall announces the dates shortly before blossoming. Call the number above for more information. The trails pass through extensive wet and muddy areas; boots are recommended. By midsummer, the deep forest is the domain of mosquitoes. A walk here when insects are active is made more pleasant by repellent.

## Access

In Poland where US 224, OH 170, and OH 616 meet, head south on OH 170 for one block and turn right on College Street. Follow College Street past Poland Middle School to the end, about 0.6 mile. Leave your car in the gravel parking lot on your left.

## Trail

Walk through the opening in the fence to the left of the stone columns that flank the road entrance. The Daffodil Trail leads through dense forest but soon comes out onto Butler Circle in the vicinity of the Bremner Shelter. Turn left, following the left half of the circle, and then turn left again at the first opportunity. The Bluebell Trail curves right and descends to cross Drake Run on a wide concrete span.

The path follows Yellow Creek upstream through a lush bottom of giant American sycamores, tulip trees, and spring wildflowers. This is prime habitat for Virginia bluebell (also called Virginia cowslip or mertensia) and the spectacular springtime display of their trumpetlike blossoms has few equals. They bloom between March and May.

Stay on the main trail where a narrow side trail goes right at a picnic table. Fork left where the trail splits to stay close to the creek. Pass a bridge over the creek and keep straight on the Bluebell Trail. After the way circles back in a hairpin curve to the right rear, watch for a narrow footpath that goes to your left, the Tornado Trail. All of the hiking trails in the forest are marked by small, greenish metal squares nailed to trees.

*Poland Municipal Forest protects 250 acres in the Yellow Creek watershed.*

Cross a small run. Keep straight where the more obvious Big Willow Trail, also marked with greenish squares, goes right. Boardwalks lift you above the low areas in the forest. Turn right on the next path, the Trillium Trail, where the Tornado Trail continues straight through a dense tangle. The Trillium Trail, as its name suggests, passes a part of the forest noted for large-flowered or white trillium, the state wildflower and the showiest of the eight species of trillium found in Ohio. The peak blooming time is between April and June.

Reach the straight, wide Butler Trail and turn right. The Butler Trail follows an old road through the forest. After descending slightly to cross Drake Run, turn left on the narrow Drake Run Trail. This path soon curves right and becomes the East Beechwood Trail. The way passes through a mature upland forest of American beech, black cherry, basswood, and sugar maple. Large-flowered trilliums are common.

Come upon the broad McKinley Trail and turn right. Soon cross the Butler Trail and continue straight on the Gutknecht Trail. The way leads along the northern border of the municipal forest directly to College Street. Turn right and you soon reach the parking lot.

# Books from The Countryman Press and Backcountry Publications

The Countryman Press and Backcountry Publications, long known for fine books on travel and outdoor recreation, offer a range of practical and readable manuals.

## Walks & Rambles Series

*Walks & Rambles in Southwestern Ohio*
*Walks & Rambles on Cape Cod and the Islands*
*Walks & Rambles in Dutchess and Putnam Counties*
*Walks & Rambles in Westchester & Fairfield Counties,* 2nd Ed.
*Walks & Rambles in Rhode Island,* 2nd Ed.
*More Walks & Rambles in Rhode Island*
*Walks & Rambles on the Delmarva Peninsula*
*Walks & Rambles in the Upper Connecticut River Valley*
*Walks & Rambles in and around St. Louis*

## Hiking Series

*Fifty Hikes in the Adirondacks*
*Fifty Hikes in Central New York*
*Fifty Hikes in Central Pennsylvania*
*Fifty Hikes in Connecticut*
*Fifty Hikes in Eastern Pennsylvania*
*Fifty Hikes in the Hudson Valley*
*Fifty Hikes in Lower Michigan*
*Fifty Hikes in Massachusetts*
*Fifty Hikes in the Mountains of North Carolina*
*Fifty Hikes in New Jersey*
*Fifty Hikes in Northern Maine*
*Fifty Hikes in Northern Virginia*
*Fifty Hikes in Ohio*
*Fifty Hikes in Southern Maine*
*Fifty Hikes in Vermont*
*Fifty Hikes in Western New York*
*Fifty Hikes in Western Pennsylvania*
*Fifty Hikes in the White Mountains*
*Fifty More Hikes in New Hampshire*

Our books are available at bookstores, or they may be ordered directly from the publisher. For ordering information or for a complete catalog, please contact: The Countryman Press, c/o W.W. Norton & Company, Inc., 800 Keystone Industrial Park, Scranton, PA 18512.